The Effective Supervisor's Handbook

Second Edition

Louis V. Imundo

American Management Association

New York • Atlanta • Boston • Chicago • Kansas City • San Francisco • Washington, D.C.
Brussels • Toronto • Mexico City

Library of Congress Cataloging-in-Publication Data

Imundo, Louis V.
        The effective supervisor's handbook / Louis V. Imundo.—2nd ed.
            p. cm.
        Includes index.
        ISBN 0-8144-5072-5 (hardcover)
        ISBN 0-8144-7829-8 (pbk.)
        1. Supervision of employees.   2. Personnel Management.   I. Title.
HF5549.I48   1991   91-53059
658.3'02—dc20   CIP

First AMACOM paperback edition 1993

Printing number

10 9 8 7 6 5

The
Effective
Supervisor's
Handbook

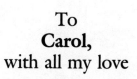

To
Carol,
with all my love

Contents

Preface

When it was suggested that I write a second edition of this book, I asked myself why. After all, the first edition was still selling well after being in print for over ten years. I thought of the adage "If it ain't broke, don't fix it." Then I quickly remembered something I have been saying for many years: "If the likelihood that it's going to break is going up, fix it before it does." I also remembered another statement I'm fond of: "If you can improve upon it, do it." This brings me to the reasons why I decided to write a second edition.

Since I wrote the first edition in the late 1970s, my exposure to management and knowledge of how it is practiced have increased. In large part this is due to my exposure to well over 100,000 people. These people work in all types of organizations, at all levels of management, and are involved in managing all sorts of activities. If I lived to be 1,000 years old, I could not possibly personally experience and learn what I have from what so many have shared with me. Since writing the first edition I have added a few more years to my life and have experienced many things. I hope my knowledge and wisdom have increased with the passage of time. In revising this book I have attempted to build upon the foundation established by the first edition.

Learning From Experience

It has often been said that personal experience is the best teacher. I have never fully embraced this idea. While, without a doubt, personal experience can be a good teacher, it can also bring disastrous results. There are some things I would like to avoid personally experiencing—most notably, death. I'd rather someone else, preferably someone I'm not too fond of, experience death and then tell me if I should exercise or hold my option card. I'd also rather someone else fail at something. In this way I can learn from that person's mistakes and avoid failure. The point is that if we learn from the successes and failures of others, we can avoid making the same or comparable mistakes; in this way, we can progress faster. There is wisdom in the old proverb: "Those who do not learn from the mistakes of the past are doomed to repeat them." While history infrequently repeats anything identically, situations all too frequently recur in a comparable or parallel way.

The idea of learning from the successes and failures of others is applicable to the study and practice of management. The history of the world is very much the history of management as applied to human activities. We can learn much from the past and apply it to the present and future. This is not to say that following identically what has led to past success is a guarantee of future success. The degree to which present and likely future conditions differ from the past must be recognized and considered when making current decisions. The more present conditions resemble the past, methods that lead to success—especially if time tested—can be reapplied, sometimes with little if any modification. The more present conditions differ from the past, the less likely past methods will work. Therefore, a key element in practicing management is to recognize the degree and extent to which past, present, and projected future conditions differ.

This is easier said then done, however. All too often present-day practitioners of management believe that nothing in the present in any way resembles the past. While the present is not identical to the past, there is more in common than most people realize. Too many managers fail to check what their predecessors in organizations, be they government, commerce, industry, religion, or military, have done in comparable situations. This is a major reason why today's leaders are more likely to make mistakes that could be either reduced in severity or avoided.

Another potential problem of learning from personal experience is that some people don't learn; they keep making the same mistakes over and over again. How often have we heard someone say, "I've been doing this for over twenty years and have survived"? In some cases the person has survived in spite of him or herself. There are also situations whereby if people changed their established ways, they could achieve better results. And then there are instances in which people know that what they are doing is wrong, but either cannot or will not change.

Now that I have punctured the idea of personal experience as a good way to learn, let me do a little backtracking. With proper guidance, personal experience *can* be an effective way to learn; it's just that it often takes so much time. A central theme of this book is that if you can learn from what I have written, which is based on my personal experiences and the experiences of over 100,000 others who practice management, then you can build on this knowledge, avoiding mistakes that predecessors have made and progressing faster and further.

I have written this book so it can be used by supervisors in any type of organization with all levels of employees. It can be used by managers who supervise attorneys, physicians, scientists, engineers, educators, electricians, carpenters, machinists, office personnel, and factory employees. Because the book has been written for supervisors in any type of private or public organization, the use of the word *company* has been carefully avoided. In its place the word *organization* has been used. Another word that has been carefully avoided is *subordinate*. To me, *subordinate* communicates an image of an indentured servant. In its place the word *employee* has been used. Employees are not indentured servants; they are people who voluntarily join organizations and contribute their skills and energy in return for certain rewards and benefits from the organization.

Learning to Apply Management

Management is the key activity that separates successful organizations from those that fail. To apply management successfully to different organizations and situations, it is important to recognize that each environment or situation has a degree of uniqueness. If that uniqueness is not recognized and taken into consideration, the application of management that has worked in one environment or situation may not work in another. Many writers and practitioners of management have failed to recognize this and have erroneously concluded that management has only limited applicability.

Some time ago I came to the conclusion that no distinct body of knowledge called *management* exists. Management involves virtually every discipline from anthropology to zoology. No one could deny that management involves a great deal of psychology, sociology, and applied philosophy. The laws of biology pertaining to excessive inbreeding and emergence of recessive, often abnormal traits can also be readily applied to organizations. For instance, excessive inbreeding—that is, exclusive promotion from within—usually weakens the gene pool and produces mutant managers who can't manage competently. Management also involves a lot of economics and, to varying degrees, religion. Additionally, management involves the application of history, political science, and English. The list of fields of knowledge that affect and effect the practice of management is quite large.

Learning to successfully practice management is somewhat like learning to become a great chef. Without formal or informal training, a person who wanted to become a chef could conceivably spend a lifetime attempting to cook and never learn very much. Not knowing about ingredients, cooking techniques, or technology, the aspiring chef would learn only through trial and error. Conceivably, the aspiring chef could get lucky and stumble on some formulas that worked. On the other hand, if he or she received good formal and/or informal training, the learning could and most likely would be greatly accelerated.

If two aspiring chefs receive the same quality and quantity of training, is it likely they will both achieve the same level of success? No. Let us assume for a moment that one of the chefs has a moderately successful career, while the other achieves recognition as one of the world's greatest chefs. What distinguishes a moderately successful chef from a great chef? What distinguishes an average manager from a great manager? Why is it that some people become very successful while others struggle to just get by? Assuming comparable training, is the answer luck, drive, or ambition? It may be all of these, but it is mostly a matter of desire—and an understanding of how to apply specific skills under varying conditions and circumstances. This requires knowledge, perceptiveness, and a sense of timing. Without an ability to sense opportunity and the need to change, coupled with knowing how and when to act or react, failure will occur. If a person does not believe in him or herself and aspire to greatness, greatness will never be achieved. While the moderately successful chef will follow recipes to the letter and get good results, the great chef will sense differences in the environment and modify the recipes as the situation requires.

The intent of this book is to help you develop a keener insight into how management is practiced. The more you learn about organizations and people, and how they think, act, and react, the sharper your insights will become. Then you will be able to read situations better and respond and/or adapt to them.

—Louis V. Imundo

1

Management and the Supervisor's Role

Many people have long sought to define *management*. As a result an assortment of definitions have come forth, the most popular being:

- Management is getting things done through people.
- Management is planning, staffing, organizing, directing, and controlling.

I believe management is a process that involves many varying activities. It does not always involve people, although such is frequently the case. To varying degrees management involves planning and staffing, among other aspects. To me, the management process embodies the following:

- It is a process of influencing and persuading, which in reality is manipulating.
- It is a process of judging and decision making.
- It is a process of discrimination.

In order to competently manage, one must be able to apply knowledge from many different fields in varying situations.

The Process of Manipulating

Much of the literature about management covers in depth its functions or activities, usually identified as planning, staffing, organizing, directing, and controlling. Discussions of these functions often fail to capture the essence of the management process. Supervisors, as creators in part of environments, exert influence over people through formal and informal means. Supervisors are, in effect, manipulators. Many people confuse manipulation with exploitation. When we are persuaded or influenced to do something we don't want to do and we benefit from the experience, we don't feel we've been manipulated, even though we have been. When we are persuaded to do something we don't want to do and we do *not* benefit from the experience, we often do feel we've been manipulated, when in reality we have been exploited. Normally, we tend to avoid situations, conditions, activities, relationships, and experiences from which we do not benefit. In order to be effective, supervisors must have the skill to influence—that is, to manipulate—people in a positive way for the mutual benefit of employees and the organization.

Supervisors need to remember that over time all people keep a mental scorecard on the status of their relationships. If people feel they are profiting by a relationship—that is, the positives or rewards outweight the minuses or costs—they will be motivated to continue the relationship. But if, over time, they feel they are losing—that is, the minuses outweight the positives or the losses outweight the gains—they will be motivated to reverse the situation or cut their losses. Perceptions of whether one is benefiting or losing is a state of mind, and regardless of how anyone else may see a situation, it is an individual's personal assessment. Although not everyone keeps score on a moment-by-moment basis, many do. Their motto is: I DON'T GET MAD, I GET EVEN.

Supervising people should not be thought of as a popularity contest. Occasionally, supervisors must make or carry out decisions that are not well received by others. To the persons adversely affected, this is a loss, a minus—a well-received decision is of course a gain, a plus. When people perceive that the minuses outweigh the plusses, a net negative situation exists and they feel taken advantage of, or exploited.

$$\text{Benefits } (+) > \text{losses } (-) = \text{net gain } (+)$$
$$\text{Benefits } (+) < \text{losses } (-) = \text{net loss } (-)$$
$$\text{Exploitation} = \text{net loss } (-)$$

Each of us has a different tolerance level, and that level varies with situations and changes over time. If we feel sufficiently exploited, at some point we will be motivated to do something about the negative situation. That something is revenge, retaliation, or retribution. It is influenced by two variables, desire and time.

$$\text{Desire} \times \text{time} = \text{revenge}$$

Desire is not constant. We may be furious at one moment and soon thereafter forget why. Or our anger may build up over time. As desire goes up over time, the incentive to seek revenge goes up and vice versa.

Revenge can take myriad forms. People can be very creative when it comes to getting back. Sometimes just walking away from a situation is an effective form of revenge. I have been told that the opposite of love is not hate, but indifference. Just walking away and saying nothing—that is, imploying that "you are not even worth my hating you"—is a very effective way to deal with someone who rejects you. However, even if people feel sufficiently exploited to seek revenge, the opportunity to do so may not be at hand. Sometimes we have to wait for an opportunity to occur or wait until one can be created. This introduces another variable into the equation—the Imundo factor, or simply an interest payment for the delay incurred in getting revenge.

$$\text{Exploitation} = \text{revenge} + \text{interest}$$

Interest is kind of like putting salt on an open wound or giving a twist or two to the proverbial knife in someone's back.

While the notion of getting revenge does not apply to everyone all the time, supervisors should certainly consider the consequences that result over time from how they are perceived by others. Supervisors are in a difficult position because they must occasionally make or carry out unpopular decisions, which may eventually spark retaliatory responses. However, they must also get and maintain cooperation, and ultimately productivity, from those they supervise. Given the increasing demands placed on supervisors to increase productivity while keeping costs down, pressure in the work place—and ultimately on people—is increasing. Therefore, supervisors must become better skilled at manipulation while avoiding being viewed as exploiters.

Cornerstones for Effective Supervision

Effective supervision, like a solid marriage, depends on developing the essential cornerstones of trust, competence, fairness, respect, and confidence.

Without these cornerstones, you will be managing on an unstable platform. These cornerstones are not created in an instant, but once in place, they are not easily moved or destroyed.

Trust

Early in life we face the dilemma of whom to trust. We are told to trust our parents but not strangers; to trust our teachers, but not the person who offers us candy and wants to take us for a ride. The person who trusts nobody is a hopeless cynic, whereas the person who trusts everyone is a hopeless victim.

Without trust, supervisors must resort to fear, coercion, or intimidation to get cooperation. Obviously, these methods should not be the first choice. If employees do not trust their supervisors, everything that goes on between them is viewed with suspicion and mistrust. Supervisors and employees alike will look for hidden agendas and ulterior motives. Such attitudes, especially when continually present, create self-fulfilling prophecies. If we look for ghosts long enough, eventually we will convince ourselves that we've seen one. This confirms previous suspicions and attitudes become entrenched.

In our society, and for that matter to varying degrees in all societies, there are people who will take advantage of the ignorant or overly trusting. Although fortunately this characterization does not apply to most people, circumstances and conditions can cause good people to do bad things. Most people, after being taken advantage of a few times, become more cautious and wary. It is not uncommon for employees who, for whatever reasons, have come to believe they cannot trust those in authority. Conversely, it is not uncommon for supervisors who have had more than their fair share of problems with untrustworthy employees to become wary of those they supervise. This is not to imply that such is the norm in supervisor-employee relations. However, the majority of supervisors have, on occasion, had to deal with an untrustworthy employee or one who does not trust them.

So how do you establish a reputation of being trustworthy? The answer, rather simple in theory but a little harder in practice, is, *do not lie*. It is better to say nothing than to lie. Once you start lying, you must spend a lot of time covering your tracks and engaging in deception and duplicity. Also, most people are poor liars. Their nervousness is usually easily detectable by those who know them. Then, of course there is the problem of getting caught in a lie. Instead of admitting a lie was told, too many people will deny it and cover up. And last, there is the problem of some liars having lied so often that they no longer know where the truth ends and the lies begin. These problems can be avoided by simply telling the truth or saying nothing at all.

Of course, telling an occasional little white lie or shading the truth is acceptable in some instances, especially when feelings can be seriously bruised. However, there are two potentially serious problems with frequent truth shading. First, once accustomed to telling little lies, it may be easy to increase the size of the lies one notch at a time. In time, little lies grow to become big ones. Second, one can earn a reputation as being insincere and/ or a phony.

Supervisors with a reputation for being straightforward and honest occasionally bruise feelings, but have earned a reputation for being trustworthy. Knowing when to say something, carefully choosing your words, and on rare occasions telling a little white lie will reduce the likelihood of injuring feelings. Trusted supervisors find that employees are more likely to be open and honest with them.

A reputation for being trusted is something that is earned over time. And actions speak louder than words. Employees judge supervisors by how they perceive them over time. Once a person is highly trusted, that trust is not easily lost. Remember, trust is part of the moral fabric of any organization or society. People in leadership positions must be trusted if they expect to be followed. Distrust cuts into the social fabric that holds organizations and societies together.

If trust is lost, can it ever be regained? The answer is yes and no. A long time ago I learned that you cannot successfully argue with a closed mind, or no mind at all. On the other hand, if a person is willing to open the door, even just a crack, you have an opportunity to regain trust. Nevertheless, the road back is a long one. Trust is sacred, and when we lose confidence in someone we have highly regarded and trusted, we're not likely to quickly trust that person again. Loss of trust is a deep wound that does not heal quickly.

Competence

Competence is a two-sided coin. To be effective, supervisors need to be perceived as competent by their supervisors as well as by the majority of employees whose work they supervise.

It is important for supervisors to understand their job requirements and performance expectations. Too often new supervisors have little real understanding of what their job entails and what performance levels are expected. The job becomes a learn-as-you-go experience, which is not all that bad considering that, in an organization subject to frequent change, job requirements also frequently change. However, the less understanding a supervisor has about job responsibilities and requirements, the greater the likelihood that either no initiative will be shown or the supervisor will make mistakes. Therefore, it is important that supervisors have some sense of direction to their jobs. They should not wait for the boss to explain what the job entails; if the information is not provided, they should seek it out. A basic understanding of one's job duties and responsibilities is requisite for being perceived as competent by one's boss.

Supervisors, like everyone else who is judged by others, need some idea of what is considered good versus acceptable versus unacceptable performance. If you are not told, ask. It is unrealistic to expect a totally clear picture, but you should have a reasonably clear understanding that will become clearer over time through feedback. Without understanding what is expected, you can spend a lot of time worrying about how you are perceived. Also, serious communication problems can arise because of misperceptions about performance. If you are perceived as being competent and are told so, you will have more self-confidence.

The other side of the competence coin is your employees' perception of your competence. Obviously, if the majority of your employees view you as incompetent, support and cooperation will dwindle. Unfortunately, it is still far too commonplace for employees to view their supervisors as incompetent because of a serious misunderstanding about the supervisor's role. There is still a strong tendency among employees to believe a supervisor should have more technical expertise than the employees who actually do the work. For instance, if a supervisor's job is to have as much technical expertise as the people he or she supervises, then when an employee asks for guidance on a technical problem, the supervisor should be able to give same. Repeated failure to be able to give answers or insight will lead to perceptions of incompetence. In some supervisory jobs such a requirement exists; this is particularly true of so-called working supervisors.

If a supervisor is expected to perform managerial activities typical of first-level management, and has ten or more employees to supervise, it is unrealistic to expect someone to be a competent manager and also maintain technical competence. This notion becomes even more ridiculous if the supervisor is overseeing the work of a number of people, each of whom has a unique, highly developed skill. For example, if the boss should understand more about the work each employee does, then the CEO of Procter &

Gamble would know more about every job under his supervision than the employees actually doing the work.

To reduce the likelihood of role misconceptions, you first need a fairly clear understanding of your role and then to share this information with the people you supervise. If it's your job to be a full-time first-level manager, and not to maintain the highest level of technical competency, then tell your employees. Then when they ask you for technical guidance, if they even ask at all, they will not be surprised when you do not have an answer, or you refer them elsewhere.

It is possible that someone is competent in his or her job, but untrustworthy as a person? Yes. This type of person is dangerous to work with or be around. Is it possible that a person is incompetent in his or her job but basically trustworthy as a person? Again, yes. The best condition is when both trust and competence exist at a high level.

I have often asked supervisors the following question: In terms of promotion in the organization, which is given higher weight—trust or competency? Typically, inexperienced, often younger supervisors say competency while experienced, often older supervisors cite trust. Who is right? The correct answer is trust. In the overwhelming majority of cases, higher weight is accorded to trust, for good reason. Incidentally, trust is also synonymously called being a team player. As people move up in an organization their power and authority usually expand. Total authority vested in one person is, of course, an exception. A person with considerable power and autonomy who cannot be trusted presents a potentially dangerous situation—a potential rogue or loose cannon. This is the primary reason why the most important positions of authority in Japanese companies with operations in the United States are reserved for Japanese managers. Japanese top managers simply do not trust U.S. managers. If the conditions were reversed, I doubt if U.S. managers would act any differently. The trust simply is not there yet, and will take time to develop.

If an organization is tightly run by a single, highly capable person, then trust is likely to be much more highly valued than competence. The management philosophy runs along the lines of, "I'll tell you what to do, you carry it out." What this person wants are people who are highly trustworthy and not overly capable of thinking. Furthermore, they are less apt to question. The problem is, of course, what happens when the all-knowing, all-seeing boss moves on. Unfortunately, the successor is likely to be brain dead if promotions have been based almost exclusively on trust and the escalator principle. (The escalator principle is promotion by finding one's place on the escalator and moving up as others leave by resignation, retirement, or death.)

Unfortunately, far too often, and more frequently in large organizations, too much weight is given to trustworthiness and too little to competency. Many organizations in this country, especially the large corporations, have too many people in high management positions who are far more trustworthy than competent. This is the major reason why so many large corporations are foundering in the rough seas of global competition.

Trust should be balanced with competence. On rare occasions, competency is given higher weight, however very competent people who are not trusted usually last just long enough for the boss to get the necessary knowledge from them. They are just too dangerous to keep around unless they can be closely watched. Instead, organizations need trustworthy, competent people in managerial positions at all levels.

Fairness

The more employees perceive they are being treated unfairly, the less likely they are to willingly cooperate with their supervisors. Perceptions of fairness and unfairness are relative and, of course, reflect a state of mind. While each employee's personal perception is unique, when people have similar values their perception of what is fair and unfair will be similar also. Though our society is quite diverse, values are pretty much the same from region to region. For instance, whether in the Southeast or the Northwest, most people become outraged when a criminal gets away with something. They also think it unjust when two employees get into a fight and both are fired, though one was clearly the aggressor and the other an innocent victim.

While supervisors are required to manage within a framework of organizational policies and procedures, they usually have a fair amount of latitude in dealing with employees. A clever supervisor can go by the book, making an employee's job life miserable while operating within the policies and procedures designed to protect employees from misuse of power. As pointed out earlier, if employees believe they are being treated unfairly, they can find creative ways to retaliate, often without getting caught. If supervisors do the same, a vicious circle of embattlement and entrapment develops. Remember the Golden Rule: Do unto others what you would have them do unto you.

Because of constraints, pressures, value, and perceptual differences, on occasion even the best supervisors will be viewed as unfair. This is why supervisors should explain why they are taking certain positions or making certain decisions. It need not be done every time, but should be seriously considered when major decisions are made affecting individuals or the group. Supervisors should also listen to the reasons why employees believe they are being treated unfairly. Be prepared, if it is within your scope of authority, to correct an injustice.

History has clearly proved that unchecked power leads ultimately to power misused. This applies to organizations as well as societies. No supervisor likes to have a decision rescinded by higher authority, and yet, because egos get in front of brains, some supervisors will not admit they were wrong and make amends—even when they know they were wrong. If no due process exists within the organization, supervisors are more likely to be perceived as misusing their authority, since they do not have to fear their decisions will be challenged or that employees have a sanctioned system of appeal. And worse than no system of reviewing managerial authority is the review system that does not work. A failed system is one in which higher-level management never reverses lower-level management, no matter how wrong the decisions may have been.

The law, top-level management's philosophy, training of managers, and how managers get rewarded and penalized interplay in establishing a climate of fairness. What maintains that climate over time is how employees feel about the way they are treated and what forums exist to settle differences. With respect to fairness, the best test of a supervisor's managerial skills is for employees to have the unrestricted right, free from fear of reprisal, to present their views on perceived mistreatment. This is commonly known as organizational due process. In unionized organizations, it is the grievance procedure. Sometimes separate grievance and appeals systems exist. In nonunion organizations, due-process forums are known by a variety of labels, such as Open Door Policy, Employee Speak-Out Program, I Have a Concern, or Let's Talk.

All such forums, at least in theory, are designed to maintain an overall climate of fairness. When an employee expresses a concern through an established mechanism, whether formal or informally, the individual gets his or her day in court. If the supervisor is judged to have erred, amends are made and the supervisor has an opportunity to learn from the mistake. If the supervisor is supported, the supervisor's behavior is reinforced. In either case, aggrieved employees have an opportunity to present their position. What makes such systems work is a desire on management's part to treat employees fairly, a willingness to admit mistakes when such have occurred, and a desire to make necessary amends or take corrective action. Except for unusual or extraordinary reasons, all forums for due process, whether formal or informal, should start with the supervisor.

Respect

Never intended as a poularity contest, supervision has always been demanding, and in today's world has become even more demanding. Supervisors are told to practice good human relations, but are concurrently told that production cannot suffer. What it so often comes down to is: Maintain productivity and if you have any time left over use it for human relations. Supervisors who continually push for increased output, higher quality, and lower costs and who find no time to practice good human relations will suffer a loss of respect. Supervisors who frequently misuse their authority, regardless of whether due process exists for employees, will not have employee respect. Supervisors who make little if any demands on employees may be popular, but likely will not be respected. So how does a supervisor earn respect?

Initial respect from employees may be easily acquired, but maintaining respect has to be earned. Your basic attitude toward people in general—and toward the people you supervise specifically will certainly influence how you deal with people and employees. Supervisors who distrust and dislike people will find it difficult over time to hide their feelings. People can usually sense when someone distrusts and/or dislikes them; when this is sensed, employees either minimize interaction or act defensively to protect themselves. How you treat employees over time, and how employees perceive they are treated, will strongly influence the respect you receive. If you who have a basic respect for people, respect employees, and strive to treat them fairly without seriously affecting productivity, quality, or costs adversely, you will find yourself getting and keeping your employees' respect. The best reputation a supervisor can have is to be known as a demanding person who is also fair, sensitive, and compassionate.

Confidence

When mutual feelings of trust, competence, fairness, and respect exist, mutual confidence will evolve. Supervisors who have found they can highly trust employees, know they will do a credible job, deal with them openly and fairly, and respect them as human beings and employees will find that most employees are likely to feel the same about them. Trust, competence, fairness, respect, and confidence are the cornerstones for developing meaningful and productive working relationships.

Supervisors Are Managers

Supervisors are often thought of as different from people called managers. This is a pervasive and enduring misconception. For example, organizations attempt to segregate levels of management by titles. People at the highest levels are usually referred to as executives or top management. In middle levels, the array of titles is bewildering. At the first level, people in managerial positions are commonly referred to as supervisors or foremen. (The term *foreman* is sexist, and is used less now because many first-level managers are women).This artificial, and many times unnecessary, segregation of managerial levels and roles has led to considerable misunderstandings about the management process itself.

People in managerial positions, regardless of their titles, are managers, and all managers engage in similar activities. While there are, or at least should be, differences between the duties of first- and top-level managers, there are also considerable similiarities. The difference is often in the focus and depth of the activities. Whereas a supervisors' activities primarily center on people, the activities of higher-level managers involve not only people but also markets, timing, events, technology, equipment, and internal and external systems.

Managers engage in such activities as supervising, administrating, persuading, planning, training, developing, and controlling. Supervisors, depending on their organizational role, many engage in many or all of these activities, however their primary responsibility is getting people to cooperate in meeting explicit organizational goals within the set time and cost constraints. Because of changing values and attitudes and changes in the law, coupled with increased demands on organizations, getting people to cooperate to meet job-performance demands and contribute to organizational goals requires considerable skill and effort. For a variety of reasons, the demands on supervisors are likely to increase.

Supervising people is with little doubt the most complex and difficult aspect of managing. Today as probably never before the supervision of people at all organizational levels is facing intensive challenges, with greater attention and emphasis. One of the most significant reasons for this is the organizational downsizing that has recently been taking place. In the 1970s and the 1980s, organizations, under the illusion of promoting people, created far more levels of management than were really needed. Aside from driving up overhead costs and creating unnecessary activities, these extraneous layers served to both frustrate and protect supervisors. Competent supervisors often found their authority circumscribed by too many people above them. They also often could not get clear direction or decisions because of factional in-fighting. The situation reminded me of the old proverb TOO MANY COOKS SPOIL THE BROTH. Accountability and responsibility were, to a large degree, lifted from the shoulders of supervisors and placed on groups and committees. When economic necessity demanded that organizations go on a diet and get rid of their middle-age spread, many levels of management whose activities did not contribute to the organization's mission simply disappeared. As a result, the proverbial monkeys were lifted off the backs of remaining supervisors and they were given more authority to make decisions. This greatly benefited competent supervisors. Also, supervisors could not as readily shift responsibility to groups and committees. This, too, benefited competent supervisors. Incompetent supervisors no longer had readily accessible people or places to hide behind. Their incompetency was more readily detectable, and downsizing has meant trouble.

Supervisors, whether dealing with factory, office, retail store, technical, field, or so-called professional employees, are the direct link between the managerial and the operative structures of any organization. To most employees, the immediate supervisor represents "the organization." Feelings about the organization, or about members of management, their jobs, and interpersonal relations, are to varying degrees all affected by the relationship employees have with their immediate supervisor. When, from a management viewpoint, employees develop less than desirable attitudes toward others, it eventually will adversely affect cooperation and productivity. Supervisors are, therefore, in a unique position to have a direct and visible impact upon organizational productivity, costs, quality, and image.

Should You Be a Supervisor?

No one can conclusively answer that question for someone else. However, a better understanding of oneself, coupled with a greater understanding about what supervision entails, can help you decide if supervising people is for you. When I was growing up I saw so many adults who were either unhappy in their jobs or had resigned themselves to accepting what they were doing as the best they could make of their careers. Sometimes they were very frustrated and unhappy people, and it was reflected in their behavior on and off the job. Some masked it rather well, although the dissatisfaction usually found a way of surfacing. Still others found satisfaction in life outside of work to compensate.

People who do not like what they do to make a living are not apt to be as productive as people who like what they do and where they do it. Changing employers is usually far easier to do than changing careers. In theory, if a person is unhappy with his or her career, a change can and should be made; in reality, this is not so easy to do. When we are young we generally have more options and nearly always more time. As we age, options and time generally decrease. It is easier for a single twenty-five-year-old to change careers than it is for a forty-five-year-old with three children in college and mortgage payments.

Why do people go into supervision? My high school guidance counsellor asked me, at the tender age of seventeen, what I wanted to do for the rest of my life. When I could not give him a definitive answer, he made me feel as if there were something wrong with me. Most people at that age do not have specific career goals and precise timetables for achieving them. I did know then that I wanted to do work I enjoyed, not have to always take orders from a bunch of jerks, and I wanted to enjoy a comfortable life-style. I definitely did not have a blueprint for achieving these goals. In fact, I could not even define what any of the things I wanted from my career meant. However, I have successfully managed my life and achieved my goals. As I approach my half-century mark, one of my goals is to wake up each morning and find I am still here. I believe that any day above ground is a good day.

As most of us know, life is not a straight road. It has many bends and turns that cannot always be anticipated. Managing your life involves being able to read the road, and not going off it too often. Like so many other people, on occasion I have gone off the road—even been pushed off—however I have always managed to get back on the road. Some people believe they have planned out their entire life; a few even manage to have everything go according to the plan. For most of us, however, the further we look into the future, the more we cannot accurately see what is out there. The point is that most people do not have clear goals of becoming a supervisor and a plan on how to get into management. If you have such a goal and plan, that's great, as long as things go according to plan. One of the potential problems that people who precisely preplan their careers run into is that things don't always go according to plan. When such people find this to be the case, they can become very frustrated because they may have lost their ability to be flexible and adaptive.

Why do people go into supervision? For those seeking management careers, becoming a supervisor—first-level management—is the first step. This is not the case for most people, however. The most compelling reasons that people become supervisors are these:

- *Money.* Many organizations offer people a higher wage or salary if they go into supervision.
- *Power.* The position gives people the sanctioned right to exercise authority. This is not to imply that most people who go into management want to wield power over other people, but supervisors can give orders to others, as opposed to being on the receiving end all the time.
- *Job security.* People often have the belief that being in management provides more job security than nonmanagerial positions.
- *Boredom.* People are bored, frustrated, tired, or disillusioned with what they are doing and decide supervision has to be better. Sometimes the move turns out to be a good one, and sometimes it does not. The grass always seems greener on the other side of the fence. While it may be, the reason might be because that's where the manure is piled.
- *Prestige.* People seek the perceived prestige of becoming part of management.
- *Challenge.* People have the belief that they can do the job better than present incumbents or predecessors.
- *Goals.* Supervision is the thing a person has always wanted to do.

The aforementioned reasons are not listed in any order of importance. There is nothing wrong with going into management for any one or a combination of these reasons. However, if money is the biggest reason, you may have made a serious mistake. No amount of money can adequately compensate supervisors for the stress and aggravation that can come with the job. If you do not find satisfaction in the work itself, actually enjoy the stress, and are able to deal with the aggravations, you've made a poor choice. The more you know about supervision through internships, task assignments, filling in when the boss is away, attending workshops and seminars, formal education, and self-directed study, the more intelligent your choice will be.

What if a person finds out that supervision is not to his or her liking? Most people will not voluntarily leave unless they can save face and not suffer a loss in earnings. In reality, both are unlikely and that is why there are too many people in supervision who do not enjoy their work and as a consequence are not very good at it. People unhappily come to believe they are trapped by what are called golden handcuffs—pay, status, power, and the resultant loss thereof if they leave. They need to consider the consequences of staying in their position: If they do not perform to their boss's satisfaction, they could find themselves unemployed. A supervisor age 45 or more, or a higher-level manager accustomed to a comfortable life-style, could find him or herself in a rather uncomfortable situation if fired or let go because of a reduction in force. Also, a frustrated, unhappy person who cannot find constructive outlets outside of work will either take that unhappiness and frustration out on others or bottle it up inside until it reaches critical mass and either explodes or implodes. People who bottle up frustration are more likely than others to either one day go off the deep end, or suffer physical and/or mental illness. Some progressive organizations have recognized this potential problem and taken steps to reduce its likelihood or to deal with it constructively when it occurs.

In conclusion, the decision to go into supervision should be thought through. Supervision, whether an end in itself or a step toward higher management, should be a job you enjoy and find rewarding.

2

The Transition
From Worker to Supervisor

Unfortunately, the majority of people who are promoted to a supervisory position, or hired into it without having previous experience, are inadequately prepared for the role. Since the early 1980s, many organizations have improved their preparation of prospective supervisors. However, for a number of reasons the problem persists.

How does a newly appointed supervisor successfully make the transition and overcome the typical problems? Unless you have inherited a disastrous situation where immediate action must be taken, proceed with caution. While a new supervisor is likely to be anxious, employees in the units will feel likewise. Employee anxiety is usually well recognized, and too many supervisors attempt to deal with it immediately, head on. In doing so they make a serious and sometimes fatal mistake.

Employees will be anxious about what changes the new supervisor is going to make. So what do so many supervisors do? They stand up and proclaim that no changes are anticipated. In one short statement they destroy their credibility. Things will change, irrespective of whatever is said. Supervisors have limited authority and change inevitably comes from higher authority, or from sources outside the organization. And supervisors, just like all other managers, suffer from "deityship." They all want to leave their imprint, to make the world over in their own image. This is neither good nor bad, but the timing of those changes, methods used, and eventual results will determine the final judgment. The point is that new supervisors should not make any rash statement that will ultimately be discredited by actions. It would be wiser to say something like: "Changes will be made. What changes, when they will be made, and who will be affected have not been determined and remain to be seen." This is far closer to reality.

To successfully make the transition from worker to supervisor, a newly appointed supervisor needs to put into practice the 5 *L*'s: *look, listen, learn, lead,* and *laugh.*

There is one condition where, as a newly appointed supervisor, you should bypass the first three *L*'s and that is when you have inherited a crisis or when one's about to happen. In this case time is critical, and you must take immediate action to avoid further deterioration or to temporarily slow things down. This is akin to when emergency surgery on a dying patient is required. The patient may die in surgery, but will surely die if surgery is not done.

Look

A newly appointed supervisor has to develop a feel for what goes on in the unit. For example:

- How does the work flow? Where and how often do bottlenecks occur?
- How do people in the unit interact?
- What actually gets accomplished?
- Are there cliques? How are they structured? Are they cohesive? How do they interact with other groups?
- What is the work pace? Does it adjust to changes as needed or required?
- Do people appear to take pride in what they do?
- What is the level of morale?
- Who can be trusted? Who cannot be trusted?
- Who is competent? Who is incompetent?
- Is the unit structured properly to effectively and efficiently meet goals and objectives?
- What is the unit's image and reputation?
- How political is the work environment?

Now, some of this will already be known to a supervisor who is promoted from within. Nevertheless, look around. When you're standing on the forest floor, you see things one way; when you're in the treetops looking down, things look a lot different.

Listen

Obviously, it is important to listen to what employees have to say about how they perceive things to be in the unit. It is perhaps even more important to listen to what they do *not* say. Sometimes silence says a lot more. One of the big problems in listening is sorting out fact from fiction. This is not to imply that employees will tell tales. However, people see things the way they want to; one person's reality is another's fantasy.

One of the most common situations a new supervisor will experience is what I call "the procession." Whenever a new supervisor appears on the scene, especially someone from the outside, employees want to get a read on the new boss. They want to see where he or she is coming from and how he or she is likely to manage. It is also politically unwise to get on a new boss's bad side. The result is that employees find opportunities to visit the new boss. They tell the new supervisor who in the group they believe is competent and who is not. They profess their loyalty and tell who can be trusted and who cannot. On rare occasions, a Judas is among the visitors, professing loyalty while looking for a way to do the new boss in. This person most likely wanted the new boss's job, was never told why he or she did not get it, or if told, will not accept the reason. This is not to state with any degree of emphasis that every work unit has a Judas in the midsts. However, they do exist, and new supervisors should not be naive about their existence. But the large majority of employees will simply profess their being team players and try to get a read on the new supervisor.

Learn

A new supervisor needs to learn what's going on, and that takes time. You need to determine who can be trusted and to what degree. You need to make judgments about who is competent and who is not. You need to understand how the world around you in the organization functions. You need to think in terms of goals and priorities, and ways to achieve them. These things take time, and this is why a new supervisor should take time, assuming such is available, to learn what needs to be done, what is going on, and whether major or minor changes are needed. It is for these reasons that many new top executive officers often wait six months or longer before making any major decisions.

Lead

Employees, if for no other reason than curiosity, take notice of how a new supervisor acts and reacts. Supervisors can be influential role models. Employees judge their supervisors as people and as managers, although such is usually not openly communicated, at least not directly. Nevertheless, employees who are favorably impressed may adopt some of their supervisor's ways of dealing with people and getting things done. Employees who are unfavorably impressed will tend to reject their supervisor's ways, and even possibly do the opposite.

The best way to lead employees is by positive example. Employees judge their supervisors, not by what they say, but by what they do. Too many supervisors and higher-level managers profess to manage in ways that others would applaud, but in reality manage quite differently. Managing in a way that is inconsistent with what you say is a good way to lose credibility. Practice what you preach and do so consistently.

Laugh

Supervising people can be quite stressful. It can be especially stressful for a new supervisor thrust into a demanding environment with little or no training. A sense of humor is essential to keep your perspective and sanity. A sense of humor is something that comes from within, from how you view life. People who enjoy life, who enjoy people, and can bounce with life's ups and downs generally have a healthier outlook on life than those who are bitter, frustrated, unhappy, too serious, or inflexible. Anyone who has raised children, especially teenagers, understands the need for a sense of humor. Employees, like children, can do things that drive you up a wall. Keeping things in perspective and being able to laugh about them helps in dealing with the stress of managing people.

Supervising people, getting work out on time, maintaining quality, and keeping costs down are serious matters, but the ability to see what's really important in life helps keep things in perspective. Being able to quietly or openly laugh about things helps you cope. A sense of humor is a human quality; without it people lose part of what makes them human. Common sense tells us people would rather work with a supervisor who is human than one who has more in common with a machine.

Guidelines for Successfully Making the Transition From Worker to Supervisor

1. Recognize and believe that as a supervisor you are part of a management team. You are a first-level manager.
2. Understand that management is a profession and a craft. Make an effort to learn about it from any valid sources.
3. Develop the self-confidence that you can learn to be an effective supervisor. If you do not have confidence in yourself, do not expect others to have it in you. Even if others do, to succeed you must eventually develop it within yourself.
4. Do not supervise with a "know-it-all" attitude. Self-confidence tempered with a little humility can be very beneficial.
5. Develop a genuine interest and concern for the employees you supervise. They are not all that different from you. They have hopes, fears, dreams, and the need to pay their bills just as you do.
6. Develop and maintain a friendly but conservative attitude with the people you supervise. Remember, you are no longer "one of the boys or girls." You can socialize, but avoid doing it with the same people all the time. Occasionally, take a rain check or go to lunch with other people.
7. Avoid overfamiliarization with employees—it can, and often does lead to contempt. Decide what side of your life is private. If you drink alcohol, never get drunk around employees. (In fact, it is a good idea to never get drunk at anytime.)
8. Understand and accept the fact that, on occasion, you are going to make or carry out decisions that are not popular. Management is not a popularity contest.
9. Make every effort to treat employees as you would like to be treated. The Golden Rule still applies.
10. Don't do anything you believe is unethical, illegal, immoral, or will seriously endanger employees. This can be difficult at times because instances have been known to occur when supervisors have been so directed.
11. Be demanding but fair, sensitive, and compassionate. Do not allow your authority to destroy your feelings and concerns for employees.

12. Find someone in a higher-level management position who can act as a mentor and guide you in your professional development.

Roles and Skills Required for Effective Supervision

An effective supervisor develops a broad mix of skills and competence to play many roles. The degree to which supervisors must possess and use the skills outlined here will vary widely with job demands and responsibilities.

• *Psychologist.* Supervising people involves knowledge about human behavior. Supervisors need to be able to read the people they supervise, to a degree be able to predict their behavior, have a feel for their wants and needs, and be able to influence them.

• *Missionary.* One of the best ways to develop commitment in people is to get them to be believers. People with compatible beliefs are more likely to work together. Supervisors need to understand the organization's values, subscribe to them, and influence employees by their words and actions to become believers.

• *Salesperson.* Today, supervisors do more selling than telling. This is especially true when supervising employees who are mobile and whose skills are in high demand. Whereas being a missionary pertains to values, being a salesperson pertains to specific direction.

• *Mentor.* Supervisors, particularly experienced successful supervisors, can provide counsel and guidance to younger people in threading their way through life. Supervisors can pass on what they have learned about surviving and prospering to employees who seek their counsel. Finding a good mentor is key to upward mobility in an organization.

• *Physician.* While supervisors are not licensed physicians, they nonetheless need to recognize when employees are truly not feeling well and when they are faking it. Supervisors must recognize the symptoms of chemical substance abuse or when employees are under severe emotional strain. They must have some basic training in how to deal with these situations.

• *Babysitter.* It would be wonderful if employees always behaved as intelligent, mature, responsible adults. Occasions do arise when an individual or even groups of employees act immature or irresponsible. Supervisors sometimes have to babysit employees, to continually watch them to ensure they do not cause or get into trouble.

• *Politician.* Politics is part of human interaction and simply a fact of life. Supervisors need to know how to work with those in power to get things accomplished.

• *Teacher.* Teaching involves modeling desired behavior as well as giving guidance and instruction. Supervisors play important roles as trainers and/or facilitators in seeing that procedures is put into proper practice.

• *Clerk.* Supervision involves record keeping. Increasingly, documentation is needed to support decisions and actions. Data bases need to be developed and maintained to provide information for decisions. With organizational downsizing or retrenchment, supervisors have to manage more and simply follow orders less. Having to manage means passing judgments and making decisions, which requires accurate and timely information. Without information and the ability to retrieve it, supervisors will be more likely to make mistakes and/or unable to substantiate the reasons for decisions and actions.

• *Referee.* When people interact, conflict is inevitable. Employees get into squabbles and even serious confrontations. Supervisors need to be able to intervene and act as a referee when situations warrant.

• *Judge.* By virtue of their position, supervisors have to pass judgment on employees and the things they do.

• *Technician.* Working supervisors—those who do the same or comparable technical work as the people they supervise—need to maintain a high level of technical skills. In fact, they often need to be the experts, so when called on they can solve the difficult problems. Supervisors who spend most of their time managing do not need to maintain high levels of technical proficiency. However, the latter need to know where to find answers or be able to guide employees to where solutions or answers can be found.

• *Chaplain.* Supervisors are frequently cast in the role of chaplin, listening to employees' personal and/or work-related problems. They must also listen to gripes and complaints, or confessions of wrongdoing. In such instances supervisors need to be patient, understanding, and if necessary give advice and counsel. Supervisors are also required to give their approval on what employees do correctly.

• *Diplomat.* Supervisors have to continually deal with people's egos and feelings. To be effective, supervisors need to use diplomacy and be able to tactfully get their point across. While there are occasions when being intimidating, brusque, or abrasive is justified, such methods come with a high price. Carefully choosing your words, thinking before acting, being aware of timing, showing sensitivity to others' views and feelings, and showing a willingness to occasionally compromise will get better results. Occasionally, supervisors have to function as diplomatic couriers in dealing with feuding managers or employees.

• *Police officer.* Supervisors have to function as organizational police officers when employees deviate from implied or expressed standards of conduct, and do not quickly self-correct. It is important, however, to take many factors into consideration in deciding how much corrective action is necessary and what form it should take.

The Skills and Functions of Supervision

You have been placed in a supervisory position primarily because you have qualities and skills that enable you to effectively engage in the activities of management. One important function of managers at any level is to create, or help to create, environments where people are willing to cooperate to achieve common goals. In working toward common goals, people also satisfy their personal needs. Let's take a closer look at some of those important skills and traits.

• *Supervisors must have conceptual skills.* You must be able to conceptualize the technical and human aspects of work, understanding people, job requirements, and work environments. You must understand what motivates people, and to what ends they are motivated.

• *Supervisors need organizational skills.* As organizational goals, priorities, tasks, technology, and personnel change, the unit's operating structure should also change. Because people are territorializers, there is a tendency to make changing goals fit the existing structure rather than changing the structure. The more often change occurs, the more you need to assess whether your resources, both human and nonhuman, are optimally deployed and utilized to meet demands. Remember that the "prime directive" for creating any organizational structure is to facilitate effectively and efficiently the meeting of goals and objectives. As goals and objectives change, so should the structure.

• *Supervisors must have interpersonal skills.* Knowing individual and organizational needs is not sufficient; you must also know how to put them together. How to approach people, how approachable you are, how you interact with people in terms of influencing, communicating, and listening are all extremely important. You must develop a sense of timing. It is not enough to know what to say and how to say it, you must also know when to say it. Recognize that each human being is unique, and develop a personal relationship and approach to handling interactions with each person that enhance rather than detract from the person's desire to cooperate. Know how to tell people when they have not performed to standards, as well as when they have met or exceeded standards.

• *Supervisors have to be able to maintain control.* You must be able to exert control when the occasion necessitates it. Unfortunately, not all people do the right things all the time. People deviate from what is required or expected, out of either ignorance or intent. Supervisors have the responsibility for ensuring that requirements are met and objectives achieved. Although employees can be held accountable for their actions, the final responsibility rests with you. This being the case, it is essential that supervisors be able to impose restrictions or controls on others. In some cases minor adjustments to activities or relationships are required, while other times a major overhaul and the assumption of total control are necessary.

• *Supervisors must be effective communicators.* You are continually selling your ideas to bosses, peers, and employees. Persuasiveness, perseverance, and timing are important in selling ideas. Supervisors, like other levels of management, usually have more responsibility than authority. To accomplish goals over the long run, you must influence people to do things voluntarily rather than order compliance.

• *Supervisors must be effective teachers.* An important and often overlooked requirement of supervisory positions is the training and development of employees. Change in organizations is essential to ensure continued survival. To meet changing organizational requirements, and to give employees opportunities to satisfy professional growth needs, training and development activities are necessary.

• *Supervisors must be planners.* Planning is an essential activity of supervisors—it determines future actions. Planning requires an ability to see what needs to be accomplished and how to get things done. In the planning process, supervisors often act as internal sensors for higher levels of management. Since you are closest to the operational environment, you are in the best position to communicate the upward information about employee concerns and feelings to aid in decision making.

• *Supervisors must be doers.* They must be able to get cooperation and, within time, cost, and other constraints, achieve required results.

• *Supervisors need to be staffers.* Supervisors should participate in the staffing process. Staffing may be divided into two components: bringing people into the organization, and assigning them to the various roles and/ or jobs that are available. Unfortunately, in too many organizations supervisors have little input or control over recruitment and personnel selection. Placement practices vary widely. In some organizations, supervisors have considerable placement authority while in others, human resources personnel, higher management, self-directed teams, or unions curtail that authority. In a unionized organization, the labor-management agreement often stipulates the placement procedure. Job selection, job transfer, bumping, and promotion are other activities normally covered in labor-management agreements.

• *Supervisors need to be leaders, facilitators, and coordinators.* In recent years, in some organizations, work groups have been given more autonomy and are more self-directed. Supervisors have been given more responsibility for coordinating the activities within and between groups. Supervisors now frequently function as facilitators, coordinators, or bridges between units and also interconnect with higher management. Supervisors still have to direct employees, but today with more emphasis on work group autonomy, it's less likely you'll play the role of straw boss.

Many factors, especially personality, influence the way supervisors direct employees, and many conditions in the job environment affect the scope and depth of direction given to employees. Supervisors need to develop an array of techniques or styles for giving that direction.

Why Supervisors Fail to Be Effective Managers

Personal Likes and Dislikes Rule

Supervisors—like the rest of us—have their likes and dislikes: Clashes of personality are inevitable. We tend to associate with people with whom we are comfortable, and either avoid or are wary when dealing with people whom we do not particularly care for. In the work place, however, supervisors have to set an example and work with people whom they may not like. If you go out of your way to avoid certain people with whom you need to interact, or often find yourself in confrontations with such people, you set a bad example. Additionally, you spend more time bickering and squabbling than cooperating and producing.

In the work place, there should be little room for personality conflicts—and little, if any, tolerance for them. One of the most difficult things for people at all levels of management to learn is to separate personal and professional feelings. Supervisors have to think in terms of what those they are not fond of can and do contribute. This is easier said than done, of course. You need to understand that whether or not you like someone, you may need to work with that person. This does not mean you have to socialize to any degree with people whom you do not like. However, on the job you must control your personal feelings and focus on the mission. Conversely, you must avoid letting your personal likes cloud your judgment when dealing with people who contribute little professionally.

If you are to survive in management, you need to be able to look at someone and say, "I like him/her as a person and enjoy his/her company. However, since he/she is professionally incompetent, I do not want him/her on our team." Conversely, "I do not like him/her as a person and would not invite him/her to my home, but professionally he/she is very competent and makes significant contributions. Therefore, I want him/her on our team." Inability and/or unwillingness to work with people whom they do not particularly like is a major reason why supervisors fail.

Individual Shortcomings

Supervisors also fail because of individual shortcomings such as lack of ambition, drive, intelligence, emotional maturity, or sensitivity. Some shortcomings can be overcome by training, guidance, counseling, experience, and desire. Some shortcomings are just baggage we carry through life. Recognizing shortcomings, working at improvement, and compensating with other attributes will keep most supervisors from failing. This assumes a singular shortcoming or a combination of shortcomings is not fatal.

Lack of Total Commitment

One shortcoming that is all too common among supervisors is the failure to recognize that management is a profession, not just a job. Supervisors need to understand that management is more than a 9-to-5 job. While there is life after work, management requires a high level of commitment. This means that when you leave work, the problems are not always left at the work place. Occasionally, you'll take work home and spend personal time on work matters. In fact, the higher you move up in an organization, typically the more commitment is required. It takes considerable skill to keep a healthy balance between personal and professional life and be an effective supervisor.

Being Out of Date

Supervisors often fail to embrace the fact that, as a profession, management needs to be learned as well as practiced. While no clearly defined body of knowledge called "management" exists, much has been written about management practices. Because the demands on supervisors have and will likely continue to increase, it is essential that you continually make the time to stay abreast of what is changing in management practices. It would also be wise to have some current knowledge about their industry environment. Supervisors with a solid foundation in management can build on it, understanding their industry and applying what they know. Remember that management—like medicine, law, accounting—is a profession. Just as people in these professions have to keep up to date, so do supervisors in their craft.

Avoiding Problems

Supervisors, like anybody else, have a tendency to avoid doing what they do not do very well. If you can avoid doing things you are not very good at and succeed, that's okay. If you can delegate such activities and they are done well by others, that too may be okay. The problems arise when you avoid, or do poorly, the things you must do well. It's not what people know that gets them into trouble, it's what they need to know and do not that leads to problems. You usually know where you are deficient. The cure is to bite the bullet and learn what is required. Painful as this may be, the alternative of failure is much worse.

Confusion About Role

Another major reason for supervisors failing is an inability to perceive themselves as managers and to understand their role as members of a management team. This can be avoided or corrected by accepting the fact that supervisors are first-level managers. They are members of a family of managers in the organization. You can also take the initiative and ask for clarification of your role and guidance in living up to what is required of you.

Inflexibility

Supervisors, like everyone else, are creatures of habit: They become accustomed to behaving particular ways. Unfortunately, this can result in an unwillingness to look for better ways, experiment with new methods, or adapt to change. Older, experienced supervisors are likely to be more set in their ways, compared to relatively inexperienced supervisors who are finding their way. Like it or not, change is an inevitable fact of life. Sometimes it is welcomed, other times it is resisted. People can be very creative in either adapting to or resisting change, but failure to change when necessary is fatal. In today's fast-changing world, flexibility and adaptability are the name of the game. The sooner you accept this, the better off you will be.

How often have we heard supervisors say any of the following?

"You can't knock success."
"We've always done it this way."
"If it ain't broke, don't fix it."

Such statements should be made infrequently and with caution, if ever at all. You may not always welcome change, but overt or covert resistance is likely to be viewed as disloyalty and evoke feelings of distrust. Consider the following: Success *can* be knocked if disaster is just around the corner. Success *can* be questioned if it occurs in spite of doing a lot of things wrong. Success *can* be challenged if different ways will increase the level of success.

Having done things a particular way was fine, may still be fine, but will it still work tomorrow? Why wait to fix something until it breaks? The idea behind preventative maintenance is to fix things before they break down. Waiting until something breaks before fixing it is like driving down the highway at high speed with a vibrating car caused by a loose wheel and waiting until it falls off before fixing it. Better to fix the small problem before it becomes a major one.

It should be further noted that higher-level managers who initiate change do not want to or cannot always take the time to explain the reasons for a change. When the reasons for change are not fully explained, not fully understood, or not warmly embraced, supervisors are expected to act on the faith that these managers are competent and doing what they believe is right. You need to understand that your opinions regarding change are not always wanted or appreciated. Recognize that once a change is decided, your responsibility is to support and implement it.

The aforementioned are the primary reasons why supervisors fail to develop into effective managers. There are also secondary reasons. Major errors often prove fatal, whereas minor errors do harm but usually are not immediately fatal. However, continued repetition of any one or combination of minor errors will likely prove fatal. For example:

1. *Too eager to please.* When people become supervisors, especially for the first time, they usually want to prove themselves and show those who made the decision that a wise choice was made. The danger is in acting too hastily. Remember the five *L*s. Also, remember you never get a second chance at a first impression. First impressions can make a lasting imprint on people.

2. *Promises you can't keep.* Supervisors should avoid making promises they will be unable to keep. You need to recognize the limits of your authority and influence. It is one thing to say "I'll try," and quite another to say "I will." It is also important to point out the difference between the two to employees. If supervisors promise things but fail too often to deliver them, credibility is lost. When such occurs, you need to explain why you failed to deliver. You must also be careful about any inclinations to blame others.

3. *Blaming others.* Occasionally supervisors have to function as shields for their bosses. They have to listen to employee complaints about unpopular decisions, even though they did not make them. Higher-level managers do not take kindly to supervisors who tell employees they had nothing to do with unpopular actions and that the higher-ups are responsible. If accorded the opportunity, you may inquire about the reasons for decisions, and even question them.

4. *Loose cannon.* Supervisors must recognize that what they say to others has an impact. In general, the higher up a person is in an organization, the bigger the splash he or she makes. Supervisors who wear their feelings on their shirtsleeves, and say whatever comes to mind without considering reactions, are loose cannons or rogues. You need to think before acting, choose your words carefully, and time when you say things. This is something generally not learned in books; it is learned by watching others in action and noting their behavior. It also involves some trial-and-error experience.

5. *Doing employees' work.* Supervisors who are promoted from within and have proved themselves in nonsupervisory jobs sometimes have difficulty keeping their hands off the work they used to do. Full-time managers should remember that they are now *human* engineers, no longer *technical*

engineers. Don't make it a practice to do nonmanagerial work, and thus ignore the work you should be doing. Unless you have nothing else to do and everyone else is busy, keep your hands off employees' work. Also, keep your hands off the work unless you are training employees, or it is an emergency.

6. *Passing the buck.* Some supervisors, especially those who are risk avoiders, withdraw into their jobs and avoid responsibilities. Some develop a knack for passing the buck to others. This behavior shows a lack of commitment and an unwillingness to take initiative. Smart supervisors, on the other hand, look for opportunities to expand their responsibilities without stretching their resources too thin or overextending themselves. They also learn to help others obtain what they are legitimately seeking. Either directly assist or direct those in need of people who can assist them.

7. *Too tempermental.* Supervisors who cannot control their emotions are easy prey for those who want to make them look foolish, immature, or worse. One of the more difficult things in life to successfully learn is how to control your emotions. You can display happiness, joy, frustration, anger, and any other normal emotion, however you must be able to control these emotions and the extent to which they show. Supervisors who easily lose their temper can usually be pushed into doing so, and this often results in a serious blunder. On occasion, a display of anger, outrage, or indignation can be useful. The key to being successful is controlling the releases and timing.

8. *Abuse of privilege.* Supervisors are often accorded, or at least they should be, special privileges. Taking advantage of them should be avoided, since it only calls attention to them and will arouse jealousy and possibly resentment. Additionally, bosses tend to view this as a sign of immaturity. Learn what privileges and special liberties are accorded to you and know the limits for using them.

9. *Favoritism.* Another mistake supervisors make is showing favorites. Because effective supervision involves making judgments and differentiating among employees, charges of playing favorites are unavoidable. The safest basis for playing favorites is substantiable job performance. Basing a decision on physical characteristics, age, religion, or sex is wrong unless validated as job-related. Everyone has prejudices; you must learn to either overcome or control them. Learn about people who are different; accommodate or at least tolerate their values if such does not adversely affect job performance, and view them in terms of what they can contribute.

10. *Making excuses.* Some supervisors make the mistake of believing that authority must always equal responsibility. In the real world, responsibility typically exceeds authority. When supervisors do not accept this they tend to find excuses for not getting things done. They complain about a lack of authority, money, time, people, equipment, supplies, and whatever else. Instead, recognize that given the resources and time desired, an imbecile could get things done. Be creative and resourceful, learn to see problems as opportunities, and turn adversity into adventure.

Making a successful transition from worker to supervisor is a challenging endeavor. The difficulty of making the transition is reduced when you have a solid understanding of your role and what is expected of you in that role. Recognizing potential pitfalls and working to avoid as many as realistically possible will certainly reduce the likelihood of serious problems or failure. Making a commitment to be an effective supervisor and striving to reach that goal will result in success.

3

People:
The Key to Productivity

All supervisors have to practice management within the parameters set forth by the law, regulations, organizational practices, economics, technological requirements, and safety considerations. The degree of flexibility obviously varies widely. Within these parameters supervisors need to apply their skills in ways that influence employees to cooperate and be productive. This process is commonly referred to as motivation.

Do Supervisors Motivate Employees?

The idea of motivation is something of a misconception. Unless they control employees' minds and bodies, supervisors cannot motivate employees. What supervisors can do is influence employee behavior through the use of stimulants or incentives. When you get down to the basics of managing employees you find essentially a "carrot and stick" psychology. There are really only two very basic ways supervisors can influence employee behavior in the work place. One way is to offer positive incentives (rewards) to be cooperative and productive. The other way is to use negative incentives (controls) when employees will not do what is required.

Rewards and controls come in a great many shapes. Common sense tells us that, with most employees, rewards should be stressed over controls. However, when positive incentives fail, supervisors either have to accept what employees do or apply sanctions to convince employees that what they are doing is unacceptable and that they need to change their behavior.

If employees receive meaningful rewards from doing what is required, the behaviors that led to those rewards are likely to be repeated. If employees are denied meaningful rewards because of inappropriate behavior and/or unacceptable job performance, there's a compelling reason to change that behavior. Additionally, various sanctions can be placed on employees as controls and incentives to change behavior.

Remember that it is employees who ultimately control their own behavior, not supervisors. Supervisors can influence employee behavior through the use of rewards and costs, however. If employees get rewarded for inappropriate behavior, they have little reason to change such. Likewise, if employees perceive that supervisors have little at their disposal to reward them for their contributions, they will be less inclined to comply with requests unless they fully agree with them. In an ideal world, what supervisors ask employees to do, what they want to do, what they will do are always the same. In the real world, this is not always the case. Even when agreement exists, employees still want to profit from their contributions to the organization.

Remember, too, that the only way to get people to change their behavior is to alter the consequences of that behavior. People may change entirely on their own, or a change may be due to external influences. However, it is the individual who ultimately concludes that the costs of behaving a certain way are greater than the rewards. Unless an employee comes to that conclusion, external influences will continue to be necessary. No matter how strong the external influences are, the employee must ultimately internalize the desire to change if change is to be permanent.

The desire to change is one thing; permanently changing is quite another. Sometimes employees can change on their own, and sometimes they need some help. While employees' first obligation is to themselves, their second loyalty should be to those who have a significant affect on their welfare. The "those" should be their immediate supervisors and the employer at large. When supervisors have the sanctioned authority to reward and discipline, they have powerful tools with which to manage.

To effectively influence employee behavior, you need to understand human behavior and, more important, understand the people who report to you. In the past 100 years, a large body of knowledge about human behavior has evolved. In view of that knowledge, the techniques for applying theory to practice are at relatively low levels of development. The majority of supervisors neither have the training in behavioral sciences nor the time to properly apply the techniques that have been developed. This does not mean that you cannot or should not put your knowledge about human behavior into practice. While you can learn about human behavior from behavioral scientists by direct interaction, or indirectly by what they have written or produced, much about human behavior can be learned by living and watching people in action. The more you understand human nature and the people who work with you, the more you can:

- Understand what rewards turn them on and what turns them off.
- Predict how they are likely to react to different stimuli or incentives.
- Understand their strengths and their weaknesses.
- Distinguish between the kinds of work they enjoy doing and the work they do not like.
- Anticipate how different personalities are apt to mesh or clash.
- Adjust your own behavior to deal in positive or negative ways with your employees.

Unless you could get into each employee's head on an ongoing basis, it is impossible to completely understand everyone and always accurately predict each's behavior. Even if this were possible, you are limited in adjusting your own behavior, and are limited in what you can do for or against employees. However, supervisors are neither powerless or helpless. With the knowledge and tools you develop and acquire you can influence employee behavior and—ultimately—job performance.

Needs and Behavior

Behavior is the result of people's attempts consciously or subconsciously to satisfy their needs. Everyone has needs. *Needs* are the stimuli that trigger the motivation process, while *motivation* is the observed behavior that is directed toward satisfying those needs.

The needs of people can be identified and categorized. Considerable research has yielded sufficient evidence to show that people share a broad range of similar needs. However, the importance of a specific need to an individual, the identification of needs that cause specific behavior, and how and why people organize and direct their behavior to satisfy needs are very difficult to understand. To be effective as a manager, you must develop a working understanding of motivational processes.

Categories of Needs

No two people are exactly alike. People share many traits and characteristics, yet we are all very different. We vary physically and psychologically yet, broadly speaking, we all have *physical* and *psychological* needs. Within this framework, there is a broad set of subclassifications. Many of these subclassified needs, however, embody more than one primary need. For example, people need food to sustain themselves. Can we conclude that eating is purely a physical need? The act of eating, depending upon circumstances and conditions, may be far more emotional than it is physical. In our culture, Thanksgiving dinner is a ritual filled with symbolism. The preparation, eating, and posteating phases are usually socially and psychologically as well as physically satisfying.

Following are some subclassifications of human needs; they are not categorized as either physical or psychological, since circumstances, conditions, perceptions, and values interplay to make rigid classifications impossible:

Achievement	Physical activity
Recognition	Relaxation
Acceptance	Sexual gratification
Power	Love
Self-respect	Companionship
Respect of others	Friendship
Justice	Compassion
Protection	Freedom of self-expression
Opportunity	Peace of mind
Physical well-being	

People's behavior is shaped by a variety of factors. First, human beings are not born with the same characteristics, traits, attributes, or abilities. To a degree, the traits, characteristics, and abilities inherited in the genes directly and indirectly influence behavior. In addition, no two human beings experience the same physical, social, psychological, and environmental conditions. People are both products of heredity and products of their environment and conditioning. When people work in an organization, they bring to that organization all their inherited traits, characteristics, and abilities as well as their learned behaviors. *Learned* behaviors include anything that is formally or informally learned during a person's life. These traits, characteristics, and abilities—in the form of skills, values, personality, perceptions, beliefs, feelings, and attitudes—are influenced by environmental and situational factors with resultant observed behavior. The higher the degree of similarity in people's heredity and environmental influences, the more likely they will think and act alike.

The Motivational Process

How many times have we heard someone say he or she is not motivated? Whenever we observe this behavior, we see the motivational process in action. Motivation is the action part of a need-satisfaction cycle. Whatever needs people have, consciously or subconsciously, at a given moment will cause behavior if some sort of action can be associated with the perceived eventual satisfaction of those needs. For example, suppose someone whom you did not know calmly walked up to you and began to choke you. You might experience fear, anxiety, rage, or anger; but because you are now in a state of danger, your primary need is to reach safety. You can clearly recognize your need and the seriousness of the situation. What do you do to get to safety?

The action you choose is based on your perception of what the best one is, given your subjective analysis of different available actions and their probability of success. You engage in behavior—that is, your motivational process—until you either die or achieve safety. If you engage in one form of behavior, and it is unsuccessful, you may try another behavior. As people learn, either directly by experience or indirectly from the experiences of others, they attempt to exhibit behaviors and engage in activities that will best satisfy their needs as they see them at a certain point in time.

Much has been written about needs and whether they exist in any hierarchy of importance. Certainly not all needs have the same intensity or importance. Something that was important to us at one time in our lives may be unimportant at another time. For example, our spiritual needs generally become more important as we approach death.

Research, observation, and logic do not support the idea of a common ranking of needs for all people. There is no universal order or hierarchy of human needs. Nor, for that matter, do all people think and act alike. If such were the case, managing employees would be relatively easy. All you would need to do is understand how to manage one employee, and then you would know how to manage all of them. Fortunately, or unfortunately, this is not how things exist in the real world.

As the priority and magnitude of our needs change, our behavior changes as well. Needs interact with one another, but it is the strongest sensed needs that most strongly determine behavior. Remember that when we attempt to analyze people's behavior, we deal with subjectivity and probability, which can be reduced when supervisors have a basic understanding of behavior and understand the people they supervise.

The basic principles of motivation are the following:

- Although needs can be broadly classified, their priority and intensity vary considerable, and in accordance with situations and time.
- In the vast majority of daily actions, people are guided by habits established by motivational processes.
- Motivated behavior is directed either consciously or unconsciously toward the satisfaction of needs. It is a psychological process, not controlled by logic.
- All behavior, whether conscious or subconscious, is an attempt to gain, maintain, or avoid something.
- Motivation, for the most part, is an individual matter. However, input from other people, groups, or situations also affect a person's motives and thus, behavior.
- Since people interact, motivated behavior often is part of a social process.

In effect, people are continuously motivated to serve their self-interests. This is commonly referred to as *inherent human self-interest,* known more casually as *WIIFM,* or "What's in It for Me?" There is nothing wrong with people serving their self-interests so long as the activities and behaviors are legal, moral, and ethical.

Self-Interest and Work

The rewards people seek from work may be physical, psychological, or combinations thereof. With all behavior there is usually some potential reward and some cost. Rewards are defined as anything that a person views as a benefit; costs are anything a person views as detrimental.

Membership in an organization, whether voluntary or compulsory, generally involves some loss of freedom and individuality. When people join an organization they expect some reward for coming to work and doing their job. The expected rewards are not only the expectations at the time of hiring but also the perceived changes in costs associated with continued employment. The larger the costs, the larger the expected rewards. When the expected rewards are less than the perceived costs, some degree of dissatisfaction will be manifested. If the reward is not attainable in the short term, expectations will increase proportionally with the passage of time. This is similar to an interest charge for a loan today with the promise of repayment at a future date.

One person's reward is not necessarily another person's expense. As in a healthy marriage, both parties can profit (rewards are greater than costs) from the relationship. People work for self-serving purposes, and organizations hire people for self-serving purposes. Organizations expect people to achieve productivity goals that meld with the organization's overall goal of survival. If organizations are to continue to maintain employees, then employee contributions must be greater than the costs of their maintenance.

If organizations expect employees to make a high commitment, then an environment must be maintained where employees feel that the rewards exceed the costs. Employees and organizations thus form a symbiotic relationship: The more profitable organizations and employees perceive their relationship, the greater the degree of commitment by both. The same can be said for the relationship between a supervisor and employees. Of course, the reverse also applies. The less benefit an organization sees in recruiting and retaining people, the more inclined it will be to substitute equipment and technology for people, not make a commitment to employees, and consider relocating to a more hospitable business and/or labor climate. The breakdown of this simple relationship between people and organizations underlies much of the United States' current economic and social problems.

As participants in society, people hold memberships in various organizations. Some memberships are voluntary, whereas others are somewhat involuntary. Except for those activities or organizations where membership and participation are involuntary, people usually have the choice of withdrawing from membership. Generally speaking, work in organizations is voluntary. No one can force you to stay at a job. Although people believe they can quit anytime they want, many feel trapped in their jobs. While they have the option of quitting, it is usually not feasible or even realistic to do so. Business conditions, age, family considerations, desire to stay in a community, and other factors make membership in organizations seem involuntary. As long as people feel compelled to maintain membership, they will do so. However, what happens if people feel trapped, or locked in to their jobs, and the rewards they derive from work are less than the costs? What people tend to do is change the relationship of rewards and costs.

People seem to have an unlimited capability for finding ways to either reduce their costs, and thereby proportionally increase their rewards, or increase the rewards and in effect proportionally reduce the costs. For example, employees may put less effort into their jobs, be absent more frequently, be careless, or psychologically withdraw from their work while being physically present. To avoid getting caught, employees individually or in consort use their innate and learned skills. The result is often a hound-and-fox environment. Supervisors spend considerable time and energy trying to catch employees, and employees spend considerable time and energy attempting to divert and elude supervisors.

The Meaning of Work to Employees

The importance of work differs among people and can change over time. Work activities must compete with other interests as a means of satisfying employee needs. The commitment that employees willingly make to their jobs is a function of goals, priorities, requirements, expectations, and the relative value of the rewards of work as compared to the costs.

Membership in any organization usually involves some cost to the individual. This causes problems in a society where freedom, individuality, and democracy are valued. Business organizations are generally something less than democratic in their relationships with employees. Differences in job titles, compensation, working conditions, location of offices, positions on organization charts, and other so-called aspects of rank clearly illustrate that all employees do not have the same rights, privileges, power, and status.

Money, because of its versatility, is a convenient reward. Unfortunately, the desire for money can be relatively insatiable, while all organizations have limits on their ability to offer it. Therefore the optimum objective of any organization must be to create an environment where work is perceived to be play. It must be recognized that, for many reasons, this goal is often not attainable. Remember that the more employees see work as work, the less of a commitment they will be willing to make and the greater rewards they will expect. It must also be recognized that some needs appear to be insatiable, and many people have developed unrealistically high expectations of the rewards they should receive for working in organizations.

In many organizations, jobs in offices, factories, and stores have become highly specialized and narrowly defined. In some cases jobs have become so specialized, simplified, and narrowly defined that reasonably intelligent people with high expectations quickly recognize that there is no challenge or future. When jobs fail to satisfy expected needs, employees conclude that the relationship is unfair—even that they have been cheated. They may then be motivated to keep their commitment to the jobs at an absolute minimum and to derive the maximum from the remaining available rewards—namely, the economic rewards.

Although economic rewards have implicit psychological rewards, they can also substitute for psychological rewards. It is well known that, by conditioning, these substitute satisfiers can become the actual desired rewards. Unfortunately, also by conditioning, money—with all its economic, social, and psychological meaning—has become a highly regarded reward for employees at lower levels, and increasingly at higher levels in organizations. This is especially true in inflationary times, when expectations cannot be met and existing standards of living are threatened. This situation has created considerable problems for our society. Unionization, inflation, structural unemployment, migration of corporations, higher taxes, higher product-service costs, poorer product-service quality, high rates of turnover, disciplinary problems, and absenteeism are all related to this situation.

In an attempt to satisfy needs, employees may put more emphasis on activities outside of work. From a societal perspective, this has its advantages. However, the degree to which energy and time is spent in activities outside of work at the expense of job-related activities is important. Employees may also be motivated to retaliate against the organization for what they perceive as its exploitation of them. Even though there is a risk in retaliations such as slowdowns, breaking of rules, sabotage, or absenteeism, employees may derive such high levels of satisfaction that they will take the risks.

It should not be interpreted that, if organizations could provide jobs and an environment that would satisfy all employee work-related needs, people would cooperate to the fullest. First, needs that are satisfied at one moment may not be satisfied the next moment; priorities and intensities of people's needs can change rapidly. Second, if an organization could create jobs that satisfied all its employees' work-related needs, employees could become complacent. Supervisors must recognize that by trying to establish the perfect job, environment, and relationship they could end up with employees who may have very high morale but at the same time be nonproductive. Success in dealing with people in organizations lies somewhere between the extremes of jobs that provide satisfaction of needs and those that allow for competition, stress, and frustration. In this way, employees will be motivated to seek solutions to problems by working toward organizational goals. What organizations do *not* want is an environment where employees perceive that the best way to satisfy needs is to work against organizational goals.

As has been shown, people have diverse needs. As a supervisor, you must develop an assortment of rewards for employees who make positive contributions. The larger the array of rewards available, the less emphasis employees will place on only one type of reward.

Rewards and Costs of Work

What people willingly give up to gain the benefits of organization membership depends on many factors. What people are willing to give economically, socially, psychologically, or physically is proportional to what they expect in return. Figures 1 and 2 list many of the rewards and costs associated with employment.

It is important to focus on the rewards you can give employees, as opposed to the ones you cannot. Where authority is uncertain, either ask for permission or go ahead and use them, and if reprimanded by higher authority, ask forgiveness. The best way to negate or minimize any adverse reaction from giving employees rewards that were not fully sanctioned by higher authority is to (1) show that the purpose was to reward performance, and (2) have documentation to prove the reward was clearly deserved. If there's no sanctioned way to reward employees, then what do you do? You have to settle for what you get or use sanctions and controls to convince employees they need to change. The problem with negative incentives is that they have to be maintained continually, even intensified to maintain control and cooperation.

While employees differ with respect to the rewards they want from working in an organization, are there any rewards that are commonly sought by the vast majority of employees? There are and they are the following:

Money
Job security
Fair treatment
Doing something worthwhile
Being appreciated

These rewards are not listed in order of importance; the importance varies with the person and changes with events and circumstances.

Figure 1. Possible rewards or benefits from working in an organization.

- Money-paycheck
- Money-benefits
- Security-steady employment
- Pleasant work environment
- Physically safe work environment
- Psychologically safe work environment
- Interesting work
- Challenging work
- Recognition for performance (nonfinancial awards)
- Competition
- Sense of pride in job or organizational affiliation
- Sense of accomplishment
- Job that contributes to the welfare of others
- Acquisition of status symbols
- Prestige of position of job title
- Opportunity to be promoted
- Opportunity to learn a skill
- Opportunity to acquire and exercise power
- Opportunity to participate in decision making
- Preferred work assignments
- Use of the organization's equipment
- Discounts on the organization's products and/or services
- Opportunity to work without direct supervision
- Lateral transfers
- Exposure to key decision makers
- Receiving flowers or a box of candy
- Receiving a letter of special commendation, plaque, or medal
- Preference on overtime assignments
- Time off without penalty
- Discounts on used equipment
- Performances bonuses
- Profit sharing
- Opportunity to get additional training on organizational time at organizational expense
- Flexible work schedule
- Compensatory time selection preference
- Site visits for field trips
- Preference on office location and decoration, or even just having an office
- Sabbatical leave with pay
- Participation by invitation in special sponsored, paid activities
- Freedom to choose special work assignments
- Paid memberships in professional organizations
- Paid professional publications
- Reserved parking space with one's name on it
- Freedom to do whatever one chooses as long as it is related to organizational business
- Job sharing

Figure 2. Possible costs or losses from working in an organization.

- Loss of freedom to speak one's mind
- Loss of the opportunity to do something else
- Loss of the freedom to do something else
- Physically and/or psychologically hazardous working conditions
- Loss of individuality
- Insensitive supervision
- Too much stress
- Lack of opportunity to participate in decision making
- Lack of opportunity to advance
- Boring, disinteresting, monotonous work
- Having responsibility for the work of others
- Promotion based on anything but job performance
- Low pay/benefits
- No job security
- Unable to measure or visualize results
- Continually rotating work schedules
- Having to interact with others
- Being overskilled for a job
- Being underskilled for a job
- Long working hours
- Destructive conflict and politics
- Being subject to the authority of others
- Unfriendly associates
- Destructive competition
- No recognition for performance
- No status or prestige
- Raises based on criteria other than job performance
- Working in an organization that exploits customers
- Working in an organization that disregards the environment
- Excessive work hours

Money is a powerful incentive because in our culture so much emphasis is placed on it and it has so many uses. If you have control over merit raises, promotions, and performance bonuses, you have a powerful tool at your disposal.

The importance of job security is influenced by many factors such as employment status, marketability, family situation, and general economic conditions. In general, when the economy is doing well and employers are hiring, employees are not overly concerned about job security. When the economy is doing poorly and employers are laying off, employees become increasingly concerned about job security. If you can determine who stays and who goes, you have a powerful tool to influence employee behavior. When supervisors can be the prime influences in dismissing employees for incompetence or unacceptable behavior, they have another powerful tool at their disposal.

Regardless of what is written in organizational policies and procedures, you can always find some latitude in how you treat employees. You can go out of your way to be fair with employees and treat them well, or you can make life difficult. Clever supervisors can create the illusion they are being totally fair with employees and at the same time make employees' lives difficult.

Increasingly, employees, particularly young highly knowledgeable employees, want to feel they are doing meaningful work. Additionally, the vast majority do not want to work in organizations they believe are harming people or society. It is important to explain to employees how what they do contributes to the unit's fulfilling its purpose in the organization. It is also important to show employees how the organization's products and/or services contribute to making life better for people.

With few exceptions, employees want to feel they are appreciated as human beings and as employees. While the intensity of this need varies from person to person, you should be able to identify those who need it more. When employees do a good job, find the time and use different ways to tell them you appreciate their contribution.

While not all supervisors have the same degree of authority to give or withhold these rewards, the most likely worst-case scenario is a supervisor with control over only three out of the five rewards: fair treatment, doing something worthwhile, being appreciated. Yet even control over as few as three gives you influence to reward. If more rewards are at your disposal, they can be used to reward performance withheld or taken away when performance is unacceptable.

Recognition for performance is one of the rewards listed in Figure 1. This reward can be subdivided into three distinct classes: rewards a person gives to him or herself, rewards from associates, and rewards from management. The rewards employees give themselves are intrinsic. They are satisfaction in doing their work well and belief that what they are doing is right. When employees have pride in what they do and believe what they are doing reinforces their personal values, they are strongly motivated.

Where a high degree of interdependency exists among employees, acceptance and support by peers is another very powerful influence. Acceptance or rejection by peers often is a stronger influence than influences from management. With employees who work alone and/or have no need for acceptance, peer influence obviously is less of a factor in their behavior.

Rewards from management, ranging from raises to a reserved parking space, can also be powerful influences on behavior. When all three sub-classes of rewards are aligned, they are extremely strong influences on employee behavior. On the other hand, when any one or combination of these subclasses are in conflict with another, potentially serious conflicts can arise.

Morale and Productivity

Supervisors are inclined to believe that if morale is high productivity will be high, whereas if morale is low so goes productivity. While there certainly is a relationship between morale and productivity, the correlation is not quite what it appears. Morale is something that is more readily sensed than accurately measured. Since body and mind are interrelated, and organizational life and personal life can affect one another, good or bad morale is influenced by more than the relationship between supervisors and individual, or groups of, employees. A person who is not feeling well may be irritable at work. A person with serious emotional problems may display them on the job. A person who is miserable at work may vent some frustration at home. Even though supervisors cannot totally control morale, they can influence it.

While one would think that employees with high morale would be high producers, it is quite possible to have happy employees who are not very productive. In the 1970s many organizations operated on the "contented cow" theory. They believed that if employees were more contented, they would be more productive. What happened is that employees were spoiled and no additional performance came forth. Management did not require additional performance, and many employees found they could get rewarded without having to contribute more work. As costs went up, productivity either remained flat or decreased. When the early 1980s recession occurred, and throughout the 1980s when organizations found they could not raise revenues at will, management had to take back much of what it had given. Where give-backs did not occur, management was compelled to greatly slow the flow of rewards until productivity significantly increased.

It is quite possible to create an environment where employees are well paid, have great benefits and high job security, are treated fairly, and have little demands made of them. For most, morale will be high but productivity will be low. When people believe they finally have it made, they are inclined to want to maintain the status quo. This can lead to organizational complacency, lethargy, or inertia. When employees do not believe they have it made and are a little frustrated, they have an incentive to improve things.

On the other hand, if frustration is channeled in the right direction, increased performance can result. Obviously, when employees are very distressed and see no way to constructively alleviate the problems they are faced with, it will adversely affect cooperation and job performance. Clearly then, very low morale will hurt job performance.

Some of the ways in which you can sense the level of morale are:

- How serious is everyone? An absence of humor, or humor that denigrates, is unhealthy.
- What information is flowing through the grapevine? If it is continually negative, it is sign of ill health.
- How much griping is being done? Is it the better or the problem employees doing the most complaining? If the better employees are doing the complaining, all is not well.
- What percentage of employees are leaving? Who are they? Are they the ones management is happy to see leave, or people management wish would stay? If the better employees are leaving, there are reasons for it.
- How often are employees absent and late? A higher than normal percentage could indicate morale problems. How about so called "mental" absenteeism? (Mental absenteeism is where is it believed employees really are not sick or injured, and are attempting to create the illusion that bona fide illness or injury exists.)

If morale is low, and it is adversely affecting performance, what can you do to improve morale? Here are some suggestions:

- Recognize that high morale cannot be bought. It must be earned by relationships of mutual trust, competence, fairness, respect, and confidence.
- Unless justification exists to do otherwise, share your authority, and give employees some latitude in doing their work.
- A positive can-do attitude is contagious. As a supervisor, set the right example.
- To the extent you can, keep bureaucratic red tape from blocking employees from doing their jobs.
- Be willing to admit mistakes and make amends.
- Reward performance by financial and nonfinancial means.
- Create opportunities for employees to learn and develop.

- Encourage employees to take on responsibilities that are within their capabilities.
- Respect and protect rights.
- Provide a clean, safe work place.
- Hold integrity in highest regard.

Money as a Motivator

Money in itself has no real value. It is sought because of what it represents and because it is a convenient medium of exchange. In our conspicuous-consuming culture, what money can do and what it represents make it highly regarded. Many factors influence a person's desire for money. While it surely influences the behavior of the great majority of employees, it does not influence each to the same degree. Mostly employees want money as a reward because:

- It allows them to purchase necessities like food, clothing, and shelter. However, food, clothing, and shelter are greatly influenced by psychological and social considerations. What one person defines as minimum another may view quite differently. As minimums move up, the need for money goes up.
- Money can be used to purchase such life enhancers as quality health care or education, or be used to live in better neighborhoods where better schools are located. Money can also be used for private tutors to help students get better grades.
- Money can give people a higher degree of personal security. Having a million dollars in safe, secure Treasury bills may not bring happiness, but it can relieve a lot of unhappiness. Also, someone with a lot of money is less likely to tolerate perceived mistreatment by a supervisor or employer.
- Money can be used to purchase many of life's luxuries.
- Money can be used to acquire social position and all the potential attendant benefits.
- Money can be used to acquire power, or influence those in power.
- Money is a sign of achievement and a mark of success.

How much money is enough? That varies from person to person and can change over time. For some the need is modest, for others insatiable. Normally people will not turn down money if it is given with no strings attached. In wanting more money from employers, employees will assess the costs incurred to acquire it, and decide if it is worth it. If an employee believes he or she is making a satisfactory income, working extremely hard for an extra few thousand dollars a year may not be worth the effort. Someone who is striving to reach a higher income level as a benchmark of success, or to purchase some luxury item like a very expensive sports car, may consider any sacrifice short of death as worthwhile.

People often say they will stop being motivated by money when they reach a certain salary level or net worth. What they often fail to realize is that their consumption—their wants and needs—often increase, which motivates them to continue the struggle. Sometimes they just cannot seem to slow down. Of course, nature has a way of making people slow down; it is called death. Since making a lot of money is indicative of success, failure to continue making a lot of money could be perceived as failure.

Use and Benefits of Praise

There are supervisors who say to employees: "If I don't say anything, it means you are doing a good job." Managing this way forfeits praise as a form of recognition. Praise is something that people need, and will work hard to get from those who are important to them. It is most effective when given and received as recognition, and not seen as an attempt to control behavior.

Praise often serves as a reward and makes the activity that led to it attractive, therefore praise is an effective tool in training and learning. Learning requires differentiation between correct and incorrect responses; praise reinforces correct responses and increases the likelihood of repetition. Praise generally indicates acceptance of, and a liking for, the receiver, so it can also have a positive effect on attitudes and morale.

Supervisors must recognize that praise should only be given when it is truly earned. If given too readily, it will not be as effective or fully appreciated. Some people need praise more than others. The more you know employees, the more accurate your assessments of their individual needs for praise. Passing judgment is inherent in using praise. When one person praises or criticizes another, an unequal relationship is implied. If the receiver does not accept this relationship, the comment could be resented. It is for this reason that employees are usually more receptive to praise and criticism from supervisors than supervisors are receptive to such from employees.

Use and Benefits of Competition

Americans are very competitive people. This competitive spirit can be capitalized on and used to increase cooperation and productivity. Competition is a potentially risky tool, in that it can be counterproductive. When competition exists, the individual who wins may gain in status and social prestige, or realize some form of personal achievement. However, the loser may experience failure and possibly a loss of status. Competition, therefore, must be recognized as a means to an end, not an end in itself: Any form of competition is a tool to ultimately increase productivity and/or reduce costs. The name of the game is not to compete against one another but to compete against standards or goals. Create competition against a goal or standard whereby anyone who reaches the goal is a winner; as a result, there can be many winners. In short, it should be potentially possible for everyone to be a winner.

Competition is often seen as a threat by the less capable, and sometimes it is clearly meant to be. This is especially likely when it pertains to productivity. It is to be perceived less threatening when it pertains to attendance, punctuality, quality, safety, suggestions, complaints, housekeeping, waste, scrap usage, and spoilage. If an organization gains from having employees reduce costs, increase quality or customer satisfaction, or reduce returns, it should share some of those gains. It gets back to the notion of inherent self-interest, i.e., "What's in It for Me?" (WIIFM).

Rewards, of course, must pertain to gains. When attendance, output, or quality are far below normal, then the only reward for employees who reach normal standards is that they keep their jobs. But when normal standards are exceeded, rewards should be given. Consider the following: If employee absenteeism is 15 percent and normal is 3 percent, it would be silly to offer a reward to employees who reduce their overall absenteeism to where it should be. However, if absenteeism is brought down below 3 percent, which would exceed the standard, then rewards should be available. The assumption underlying any contest for rewarding less absenteeism is that if employees are at work and producing, the employer simultaneously makes and saves money.

In any competition the rewards should be ones that employees desire. It might be useful to ask employees what kind of rewards they would like to have. While few employees reject direct payment of money, indirect financial rewards like a chauffeured-limousine night on the town, or a gift certificate should be considered. Obviously, before you can establish such a system of rewards, you need approval from higher authority.

Another point to consider is that limits should be placed on the number of times anyone can consecutively win. If one employee continually achieves the goals, everyone else's interest declines. In this case, end the contest and get employee input when creating the next game. Remember, focus on the real purpose of competition, not the act of winning.

Understanding Group Behavior

The ultimate goal of every supervisor is to develop a cohesive work group motivated to achieve organizational objectives as a means of satisfying personal needs and objectives. The benefits of having a cohesive and pro-organization work group are:

- Less direct supervision is needed.
- Peer pressure can correct unacceptable behavior.
- Higher productivity often results.
- Attendance is usually higher.
- Quality of work is higher.
- Emphasis on money as a single reward is reduced.
- Valid input to management is more freely given and tends to be more accurate.

Peer pressure in groups can be formidable, and employees may develop a stronger identification with the group than with the supervisor or the organization. Employees in a group forgo some individuality and modify their behavior in order to be accorded social position or rank by the group. The stronger an employee's need to be accepted by the group, the more the employee is apt to conform to the group's norms, values, beliefs, and expectations.

In groups, the politics of human interaction operate. Cliques form because people are drawn together by common needs and interests. Degrees of likes and dislikes for other group members evolve, and various efforts on the part of members of the group to learn other members' strengths and weaknesses occur.

Supervisors must be able to identify the social structure of the group. They must understand how the structure evolved, how it derives its power, and to what degree it changes over time and in different situations. You should learn the techniques and approaches to influence groups either to reinforce the existing social structure or to change it.

As stated, certain factors affect a group's according a member social position. On the other side, people assess groups to determine to what degree they desire acceptance and social position. The general need for acceptance by other people is one factor. Others are the technical and social composition of the group. From a technical standpoint, they may have to work with people whose training they consider beneath or above their own level. For example, CPAs may not want to associate with record keepers. On the other hand, they may want to be associated with them because they want the higher status. Perceptions of the rewards of group membership—whether social, psychological, or economic—determine to what extent people may want to identify with others who have higher or lower status.

The social structure of a group affects its members' behavior. The more effort required to achieve high standing, the less people may want to fight their way up the social ladder. This would not be true, of course, when achieving that social standing is itself a source of high personal satisfaction.

Managing the Informal Social Structure

The best way to recognize the informal social structure of a group is to compare it with its formal structure. Examine the formal working relationships and patterns of power, influence, and interaction. By comparing what should be with what actually exists, you can develop a picture of the group's informal social structure. For instance if you determine that the existing social structure is not serving the best interests of the organization, develop strategies and tactics to change the informal social structure. Some approaches that can be considered are:

- Arranging transfers of group leaders or primary influencers out of the work unit
- Rearranging formal patterns of interaction by changing jobs, work-interaction patterns, or work-place layout
- Handling employee grievances and the distribution of rewards and punishments
- Cultivating the informal communications system either to create dissension or to reinforce the structure

When group members support and enhance the activities of one another, the group is a team. If the group is not dominated by one person, each member is free to exchange ideas, thoughts, and feelings. When an employee derives satisfaction from being part of a team, this becomes one of the rewards for employment in the organization. When employees derive multiple rewards from work, they are less inclined to change jobs, even if another job offers higher compensation.

You may find the following guidelines helpful in establishing a work group that is cohesive and pro-organization:

1. Understand the group's informal social structure.
2. Be aware of employee needs and create an environment that facilitates direct satisfaction of those needs or acceptable substitute satisfiers.
3. Give recognition and praise on the basis of merit. Merit must be carefully defined, and employees must have the right to question, without personal risk, the distribution or withholding of rewards.
4. Be approachable on problems and flexible in leadership style.
5. Establish work climates that are ego enhancing and encourage employees to cooperate.
6. Have realistic expectations of employees and establish relationships of mutual trust and confidence.
7. Stand up for employees when they are right and help them learn from their mistakes when they are wrong.
8. Let employees know what is expected of them and give feedback on performance.
9. Take a sincere interest in employee welfare and development.
10. Create a team identity by rotating job assignments. In this way, people lose some of the parochialism associated with a particular job.
11. Develop group attitudes, norms, and influences that center on cooperative teamwork.
12. Develop a team spirit and a desire among employees to compete as a team instead of as individuals.

A word of caution. The group, while being cohesive and strong, should not become so strong as to suppress individual identities. People must retain their individualism while recognizing that they are part of a team. This is a very difficult and delicate balance to achieve and maintain.

Within any group, one or more informal leaders will emerge. Leaders are important to both the supervisor and the group's members. The informal and formal organizations are, to a degree, in competition for employee loyalty. Effective supervisors can identify the power structure within the group, and manage relationships so all benefit. Informal group leaders are key people because they are powerful influencers of others' behavior. They represent the values, beliefs, feelings, and attitudes of group members; they are effective communicators; they are trusted; they instill confidence in their opinions and judgments; they best help group members satisfy their needs; and they are supported by other key members of the group. Informal group leaders may possess many of the traits, abilities, and characteristics of supervisors. While they lack formal organizational recognition and formal status, their feelings and opinions carry more weight, or generate more concern, than the feelings and opinions of others.

Employees are occasionally more loyal to the informal leadership in an organization than to the formal leadership. However, while they can influence behavior, if they speak or act outside the acceptable limits of their role as perceived by the group, their leadership position is weakened. Since in any group there is competition for the leadership role, a competitor can quickly take advantage of a vulnerable incumbent.

The primary members of a group are those most closely aligned with leadership. If the group is cohesive, primary members are the emissaries and staunch political supporters of the leaders; in a sense, they form the executive committee of the group. The next stratum is composed of secondary members, who range from those close to the primary members down to the group isolates.

A work group tends to reflect a common set of desires that may or may not be evident from observation. The common threads in a group are:

- The desire to satisfy member needs for social interaction
- The need to control the actions of the group via acceptable norms
- The need to protect individual members through collective representation
- The desire to exercise greater influence over work and the work environment through group interaction
- The desire to enhance group effectiveness by pooling individual talents and resources

Don't underestimate the degree of pressure that a group's informal political structure can exert on other employees and on the organizational structure. Research has shown that employees may fear group pressure far more than they fear organizational pressure. The same applies to the evaluation of rewards. Many employees value the rewards given by their peer group more than those offered by the organization.

In terms of group dynamics, remember that positions of leadership are not formally defined by job descriptions. They are based on status, power, and the ability to influence. Learn to recognize the attitudes, values, aspirations, and degree of influence that the social structure of a group can exert. If you do not learn to recognize and manage a group's power structure, you will never achieve the same level of effectiveness as supervisors who do. A group's special power structure can be an asset to you or a liability. Unless you want to break up a social structure, develop a cohesive pro-organization structure so that the group's leadership can act as your de facto assistant.

When the informal power structure of a group is cohesive and is aligned with organizational objectives, members who stray from their responsibilities, required behavior, or objectives are apt to be the recipients of double discipline: from the supervisor as well as from their colleagues. And discipline from one's colleagues can be more severe than that administered by the formal organization.

Within the limits of their authority, supervisors are responsible for creating and maintaining a work climate in which employees will (1) want to work and (2) be able to carry out their job responsibilities effectively and efficiently. Supervisors need to reward satisfactory and better-than-satisfactory job performance, and take steps to permanently rectify less-than-satisfactory performance and/or behavior. The key to accomplishing all of this is the correct use of a variety of valued rewards. Giving and withholding valued rewards always influences behavior.

4

Developing Teamwork

Since the mid-1960s we have been witnessing a decline in the world's strongest economy. It has resulted in a decline in the standard of living for the majority of Americans and has become a threat to our very way of life. So much has been said and written about problems and what needs to be done, yet, as a country, we have failed to act. Why? Because as individuals we have tended to think the problem is not ours but rather someone else's. When the textile industry found it could not compete by making products in the United States, it shifted production to the Far East where costs, especially of labor, were cheaper. The result was that many Americans lost their jobs. While autoworkers were losing their jobs because auto prices had dramatically increased while quality decreased, consumers quite rationally kept buying the less expensive, better-made imports.

As individuals we have been acting out of our perceived self-interest. When urban neighborhoods and school systems deteriorated, those who could afford to fled to the suburbs. What we belatedly are beginning to recognize is, even for those people who appear to have been spared or have even benefitted, ultimately everyone is adversely affected. We are all affected by seeing homeless people on the street, driving on decaying roads and bridges, tolerating poorer schools, suffering a higher crime rate, and paying higher taxes in part to pay for increased welfare and more jails. We all pay a price for illiteracy, especially when we have to train and supervise such people. We all pay a price when people without self-respect use drugs and they happen to work in our organizations.

One of the most important ways supervisors can contribute to resolving our nation's declining productivity is to aggressively build teamwork. Supervisors must perceive themselves as mini-CEOs. Don't dwell on authority you do not have; rather, concentrate on using the authority you *do* have to build teamwork. Where your authority is uncertain, avoid such decision areas, ask for permission, or request forgiveness. While the concept of teamwork is nothing new, it is currently receiving a lot of attention.

Before we can go to work on developing teamwork, or strengthening what currently exists, it is important to have an understanding of just what teamwork is. Most adults are familiar with team sports. Teamwork in sports organizations, be it a community soccer team or a professional soccer team, and teamwork in business organizations have much in common. In all respects professional sports is big business today. For a football, basketball, soccer, or hockey team to win, each player must cooperate with others and do his or her part to achieve success. Football players have to work together to score points and prevent their opponents from likewise scoring points. In contrast, when people work alone, such as in a singles' tennis match, teamwork is unnecessary.

In the work place, as methods and processes have become increasingly complex and interrelated, interdependency among employees has also increased. The need for teamwork has been further emphasized by the need for increased flexibility. In today's fast-changing world, products and services must change faster to keep up with consumers' needs and preferences, as well as with competitors' offerings. Even with so-called essential services, the packaging, delivery, and applications change.

There are two distinct approaches to teamwork: the one-person team and the participatory team.

The One-Person Team Approach

This situation, which exists more than most supervisors and higher-level managers are willing to admit, operates under the illusion that power and responsibility are shared. A one-person team leader often believes that he delegates, listens to others, and involves them in decision making. However, team members do not see things the same as the leader does. They know the leader ultimately will do things his way, no matter what they say or how they feel. They learn to play the game of illusory teamwork. When asked to express their views, they either say nothing or tell the leader what they believe he wants to hear. This approach is unhealthy and ultimately creates an emotionally unstable work environment. It is better for a leader to say he is going to call the shots than to create the illusion that others will participate in major decisions. At least then people know what their roles are and recognize their relationship to the leader.

One-person teams can be very productive if the leader is extremely competent and other people recognize and accept their roles. History is replete with examples of highly successful organizations run by one person. However, over time most organizations dominated by one person get into trouble. Some of the reasons for this are:

1. The leader leaves and her successor lacks the vision, drive, or charisma to effectively lead.
2. The most capable people leave for opportunities where their talents can be more fully utilized and recognized.
3. There's a potentially unhealthy love-hate relationship between the leader and others.
4. No one dares question the leader's judgment, and the leader has no one to act as a devil's advocate.
5. Over time, people become brain dead. The brain, like muscles, will eventually wither and atrophy if not used.

The Participatory Team Approach

Difficult to develop, since it requires a strong commitment over time, the participatory team normally evolves rather than is created.

This is a team in which power is shared and no one dominates. In the long term, this approach usually yields better results than the one-person team. The participatory team is the approach emphasized in this chapter.

What Is a Team?

A team is a blending of skills and personalities. In effect each member brings something different to the party—each person's strengths and deficiencies. If people have nothing useful to contribute to the team effort, then they are neither valued or needed by the team. Teamwork should generate a synergistic effect, whereby the whole is greater than the sum of its parts.

To learn what each employee or team member can potentially contribute, it is important for everyone to get to know one another on more than just a professional basis. Getting to know people on a personal level does not imply on an intimate basis. People are entitled to maintain a private side to their lives. However, the more people are strangers to one another, the less is known about what they can contribute, what turns them on or off, and how their personalities, skills and experiences can be effectively utilized.

Before people will open themselves up they have to feel comfortable and trust the others. Sometimes it is easier for a person to be open with strangers than with those they are close to; this is because there may be less risk associated with talking to a stranger. Even when people open up and give others the opportunity to learn more about them, they are not apt to do so all at once. Prudence and caution will be exercised. How others act and react will affect how much a person continues to expose. Building teamwork is a form of bonding, and it often takes time to evolve. (An exception to this is when a crisis occurs. A crisis can bring about teamwork, however it tends not to last much beyond the crisis.)

If a team in part is characterized by people understanding one another as human beings, and better knowing their abilities and limitations, what opportunities can supervisors create for people to learn more about each other? Here are some suggestions:

• *Go out on occasion with individuals and/or groups for lunch, coffee, or even a drink after work.* A drink after work does not have to mean consumption of alcohol. An occasional breakfast meeting could also be useful. These events should be spontaneous, lest people feel obligated and less inclined to open up.

• *Put employees who normally do not continually interact with one another on special projects and task forces.* This should be done infrequently so as not to overburden employees or too often take them away from normal job duties. It is useful to put people who do not get along very well on a project together. In such instances they need to be told they must get along and if they do not it will not go down well. Regardless of personality clashes, except for very extreme cases employees have to learn to work together. When people are compelled to work together sometimes they learn to put prejudices and negative feelings aside. And sometimes these feelings substantially are reduced or cease to exist when people learn they need each other to get things done.

• *Create the time to talk about things of common interest.* This could be subjects like raising children, sports, hobbies, family life, or just trying to make one's way through life. The recognized taboos of talk about sex, politics, and religion should be considered, of course. All of us, no matter who we are or what we achieve, simply are trying to make our way through life.

• *Organize a group picnic with families included.* This is a great way to get to know employees and their families. Throwing a backyard party is also quite useful. Organize a bowling group or softball team. A word of caution, however: Create activities where everyone can be involved and that won't seriously embarrass or injure people. Highly competitive sports can also be risky. If teams are created for sports, make sure the teams are equally matched. Volleyball is a good team activity; football is not.

• *Build cooperation through challenging activities.* In recent years white-water rafting, mountain climbing, and wilderness survival programs have been popular for building teamwork. Approach these activities with extreme caution; not everyone is physically or emotionally suited to them, though they may feel compelled to participate when such activities are sponsored by the boss. Also, some people have been seriously injured and even killed. Nevertheless activities such as white water rafting can be very useful in developing teamwork under physically challenging conditions.

• *Take time out occasionally to talk with employees on a one-on-one basis.* This should be spontaneous and when neither of you are extremely busy.

Teamwork cannot exist unless employees see themselves as part of a team, but teamwork involves some loss of individuality. The payoff is in what the team can collectively accomplish, and in being identified with a successful team. The most commonly used word in the English language is *I*. The more people use it, the more likely they see the world revolving around themselves instead of being part of a larger world. Supervisors should use the words: *we, our team, the group, our family.* Practice introducing team members by name instead of job title. All too often when an outsider is introduced to a team member, the employee is introduced this way: "I'd like you to meet my assistant, Mrs. Edwards." Putting the job title in front of the individual gives the impression that the job is more important than the employee. Using the word *my* gives the impression of ownership. A better way to make an introduction is: "I'd like you to meet Mrs. Edwards, who is a member of our team." Mentioning a job title is optional.

It is also important to share credit when it has been duly earned; it shows that everyone has contributed to the success. A smart supervisor, like a smart quarterback, learns to share credit with the team. Quarterbacks are usually the first to be recognized for the team's success or failure. A smart quarterback knows that without full support from those on the front line, points will not be scored.

To carry the analogy further, linesmen who do not perform well get replaced. However, it is one thing to do what is required and another to go all out. Employees, like linesmen, are not inclined to go all out when the team leader is hogging all the credit. Many an arrogant, self-centered, egotistical quarterback has learned humility when linesmen marginally do their jobs and they get sacked; it is also not unknown for owners to trade an egotistical quarterback who alienates good team members. Likewise, egotistical supervisors can be replaced. Share the credit.

In contrast, when things go wrong, a smart coach first takes responsibility and then behind closed doors distributes some of the blame. This is contrasted with the not-so-smart coach who publicly blames the team or specific players.

Team Qualities

Productive teamwork can exist only when there is an understanding of and commitment to achievement of common goals. Common goals provide a common focus, with the team understanding the unit's primary purpose for existing and the goals that need to be met in order to fulfill that purpose. Team members must accept the goals and believe the goals can be best achieved through cooperative team effort.

Productive teams usually share many characteristics. The more of these characteristics that exist, the more productive a team is likely to be.

Characteristics of Productive Teams

• *Openness and candor.* The less people are willing to express their feelings and be honest with each other, the more likely suspicion and distrust will exist. When real teamwork is present, team members, because they basically trust each other, will be more open and honest with each other. Obviously, tact, diplomacy, timing, and consequences should be taken into account. Openness is also influenced by the willingness of others to listen.

• *Leadership that does not dominate.* While in any group it is inevitable that leaders will emerge, leadership changes with conditions and circumstances. This does not meant that titles play musical chairs; it does mean that a team member's influence, roles, and responsibilities change as conditions warrant. When one person dominates, it often leads to repression and suppression. Also, the rest of the group may increasingly find themselves dependent on the leader's direction.

• *Decisions by consensus.* The work place is not a true democracy nor is it ever likely to become one. Certainly there will be times when the leader must dominate and either not seek input from others, reject suggestions, or override others' decisions. However, the more these occur the less likely team members will be willing to give input or show initiative. Participatory teamwork involves giving team members equal voices in making many decisions.

• *Acceptance of assignments.* It might make each of us happier if we could choose all our work, however, this is unrealistic. When people are assigned to work they do not like, they have a tendency to procrastinate, complain, do a halfway job, or push it off on someone else. When real teamwork exists, team members willingly accept assignments. They also get the work done right the first time and meet deadlines. On the other hand, if people believe they are continually being taken advantage of, they will take corrective action.

• *Understood and accepted goals.* A team needs purpose, direction, and goals. Unless these are known, members are apt to go off with good intentions in the wrong directions. Members accept the goals, even if they personally disagree with them. It would be wrong for members to pursue goals they believe are either immoral, unethical, illegal, or will wrongfully endanger others. Without acceptance, it is difficult if not impossible to get full commitment.

• *Progress and results assessed.* Teamwork requires that members be results directed as opposed to process oriented, that their focus be on what the objectives and their activities be directed toward those goals. Periodically the team must assess its progress. Knowledge of progress serves to guide team action. This does not mean that process is ignored, of course, but on a continuing basis members must address the matter of how well they are doing as a team, what barriers are holding them back, and what they can do to become more productive.

• *Comfortable atmosphere.* When scarcity exists, competition and conflict are inevitable. Some competition and conflict within a team is desirable but, as with most things, too much causes problems. In a healthy team, members essentially trust one another, and in spite of competition and occasional conflict, they get along well and enjoy each other's company. They cooperate and get more done.

• *Involvement and participation.* There are three general types of people in the world: those who do not know or care about what is happening, those who watch what others do, and those who make things happen. Teamwork requires that members be involved in their work and participate in team activities. What they say and do counts for something.

• *Debate and discussion of issues.* Continued blind acceptance is unhealthy in a team because leaders do not get the benefit of members' thoughts. When decisions are made, members are more apt to support them if they have had input and believe that their views have been considered. Debate on issues can bring up more workable courses of action or solutions to problems. Debate and discussion also give members an opportunity to see where others are coming from; this helps establish identities and shows the frequency and intensity of others' viewpoints.

• *Members listen to each other.* When people disagree they often stop listening to each other. They also tend to focus on the disagreement instead of trying to arrive at a compromise. When people realize others have stopped listening, they may act in ways that reduce cooperation. Respect for others and a willingness to listen and consider opposing viewpoints are important for maintaining team spirit.

• *Common access to information.* Information is a vital resource for getting things done. Make certain that employees have access to the information they need.

• *Win-Win approach to conflict.* Adversity must be turned into cooperation. Use the problem-solving approach with the goal that each can emerge a winner. Recognize areas of agreement and use those as a base to address areas of disagreement. Members of groups in conflict should jointly explore how to accommodate or resolve differences.

• *Relatively low turnover.* It takes time for people to feel comfortable and trust one another. When employee turnover is very high, bonding cannot readily occur, because just when people are starting to understand, trust, and feel comfortable with one another some leave the organization. When turnover is high supervisors, because they do not know who can be trusted and how competent employees are, often have to maintain closer control.

Teamwork Barriers

Sometimes intentionally, but most often unintentionally, organizations create artificial barriers to teamwork by their structure, reporting relationships, policies, and practices. Many of these barriers are deeply ingrained in the culture of organizations, and therefore are resistant to change. Removal of these barriers does not automatically guarantee teamwork, however elimination of them does facilitate the establishment, maintenance, and perpetuation of teamwork. These organizational barriers are:

• *Superior vs. Subordinate.* Most organizational written policies and procedures continually use the words *superior* and *subordinate.* These words establish an unequal relationship where the subordinate is subject to the will and direction of the superior. In a manner of speaking, superior-subordinate is analogous to the master-servant relationship. Employees are not indentured servants. They are people who voluntarily join organizations and contribute to their employers' goals if they ultimately believe it is in their best interests to do so. Referring to them as subordinates is a psychological put-down, whether or not intended; consciously or subconsciously, most people resent being cast in a subservient role. This will adversely affect cooperation and teamwork. Elimination of such language can, to a large extent, facilitate teamwork. Words like *associate, colleague, employee, contemporary,* and *peer* are preferable. It should be noted that changing language alone will not have a lasting positive effect; thought, attitude, and behavior must also change.

Team leaders should also consider how members address one another. Formality can inhibit communication and, eventually, cooperation. Being overly informal can lead to potential problems. Our culture, when compared to others, is rather informal. It is generally better for all team members to be on a first-name basis, as opposed to addressing selected members by title. When outsiders are present, more formality may prevail.

• *Salary vs. Hourly.* When manufacturing was dominant in American business, *salary* and *hourly* were primarily terms used to differentiate between employees in the plant and those in the office. Hourly employees were identified with the working class and unions, whereas salaried employees were the middle class and management. To a degree, this mentality still exists. However, with the growth of nonmanufacturing businesses and government, job levels are less clearly defined. Historically, salaried employees were not paid overtime whereas hourly employees were. Whether or not employees are legally entitled to overtime is determined by the legal definitions of job duties and not whether an employee is hourly or salaried.

Similarly, hourly paid employees almost always "punch" the time clock, whereas salaried employees usually do not. Requiring some employees to punch a time card while others either fill out a card or submit nothing implies that some members are not responsible enough to get to work on time or maintain an accurate record of their time.

The distinction between hourly and salaried employees creates a class system where one group is likely to perceive itself different and even superior to the other. This can and usually does adversely affect teamwork. The idea of eliminating hourly pay and placing everyone on salary is not unique. A number of major corporations and government took this step many years ago. In a teamwork setting it is important for all employees to identify with the organization, its leadership, and the purpose(s) for its existence.

• *Professional vs. Nonprofessional.* This is another common way to differentiate employees. Referring to employees as nonprofessional is most serious, in that it precipitates jealousy and resentment, neither of which is conducive to teamwork. It is also ego deflating and can adversely affect peoples' self-esteem and attitudes toward and about their work.

Professionalism is a state of mind, not a set of educational credentials, licensure, or experience. Certain types of work require licenses, but this in and of itself does not mean that all licensed people are professionals. For instance, it does not guarantee that their work will be competent since competency is influenced by attitude as well as skills. Professionalism is an attitude that should be inherent in all employees, regardless of their job duties. All team members are professionals and their work is important.

• *Essential vs. Nonessential.* Obviously, some members' work may have somewhat more significance when compared to others' work; this makes them comparatively more essential. However, it is important that all employees feel that their work is essential to the team effort. Elimination of the essential/nonessential labels has a positive influence on teamwork.

• *White Collar vs. Blue Collar.* This distinction is both out of date and incorrect. Today, industry has even more distinctions: pink collar, clean collar, even gold and silver collar. These labels often cause employees to identify with the "collar" group instead of the team, which may be composed of people from many different job classifications.

Some of these barriers are aspects over which supervisors have no control. They are "givens" and unless higher management makes changes, they remain. While such conditions are not conducive to developing teamwork, they are not impossible to overcome. For example, even if policies, procedures, and written communiqués refer to employees as subordinates, you do not have to follow suit. If you sincerely believe all employees in the unit are professional and essential, you can take steps to ensure that everyone is treated as such. You can reduce the notion of class differences by educating employees on what others do and how they contribute to achieving goals.

A Blueprint for Team Building

To develop teamwork, it is often useful to work from a blueprint or model. Productive teamwork require that employees be reasonably well matched to their jobs and the organization's ways of functioning. When people, jobs, and the organizational ways are seriously mismatched, teamwork is handicapped. Figure 3 is a model of the relationships among people, jobs, and organizations. Let's look at each element:

The Individual

Each employee is unique and has both positive and negative qualities. When people join a team, they bring to the job all their inherited and learned traits, characteristics, and skills. This can positively or negatively affect their working relationships and job performance. While people can and do change,

Figure 3. Teamwork model.

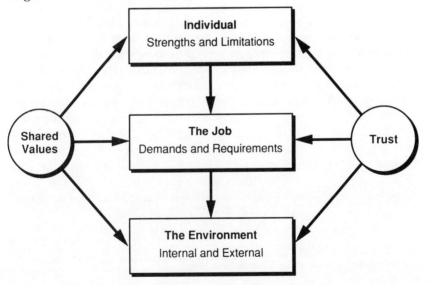

deeply rooted behavior, especially that which has been reinforced by success, is resistant to change. In some instances employees are so mismatched with the team and organization that teamwork cannot exist. When this happens, it is usually better to encourage those employees to leave rather than try to get them to change.

It must be remembered that when people are hired for jobs, the *whole* person is hired. In other words, you get the bad with the good. The more a job requires a person to use his or her mind, the more the person's personality and character will affect job behavior and performance. When hiring people it is important to know what qualities and traits, as well as education and skills, are needed to get desired performance.

The Job

Jobs differ widely. A person can be successful in one type of job, then move into another and fail. People are creatures of habit, and they carry their habits with them as they go from job to job. This is especially true of successful habits. We have all heard of successful salespersons who are promoted into management and subsequently fail in the job. This has been referred to as "rising to your level of incompetence." But this is a misnomer; the perceived incompetent is still competent at doing other work. What has happened is that the employee has failed to develop the necessary behaviors that will lead to competent job performance in the new position.

We tend to believe that effective performance in one job is predictive of successful performance in other jobs. This is true if the jobs require the same skills and the environments are similar. The more these differ, the more adaptive people must be. It is commonly believed that if a person is a good supervisor, he or she will make a good middle manager. But if the manager's job requires considerably different skills and functions under different conditions, the correlation is low and even nonexistent. People can change, however they must understand what is required and want to change. They may also need guidance and formal training.

Similarly, jobs can change because of environmental changes. When such occurs, employees may have to abandon certain ways of doing things and develop new ones. This can be difficult for some and impossible for others.

The Environment

Every organization has its collective mind-set. This is commonly referred to as its culture. Organizations are like tribes, in that they have their rites, rituals, taboos, gods and goddesses, and high priests. To survive on any team, members must learn the written and unwritten rules for behavior. As leaders change, the ways of doing things will inevitably change. Leaders will always inevitably bring about change; they may do it in either directive or nondirective ways.

Regardless of the methods used, team members must do a certain amount of adapting in order to survive and prosper. While blind obedience and conformity have inherent dangers, so does independence and nonconformity. Organizations and their leaders exert subtle and direct influences on members. Cooperation always requires sacrificing some individuality and doing some conforming.

Organizations do not function in a vacuum: They are part of society and are influenced by economic, social, and political changes. As society changes, pressures are placed on organizations to modify the ways in which they function. Organizations that are unable or unwilling to adapt face continued pressure, possible takeover, and even extinction. Whether organizations and their employees like the changes occurring in society is irrelevant. For example, many of the airlines did not want to see deregulation come about. However it did, and those that adapted capitalized on opportunities while those that did not change quickly enough were taken over or went out of business.

Environmental changes can significantly affect operations and job demands. These in turn affect the behavior of job holders and the staffing of jobs. The types of qualities needed for success in the past may be totally outmoded for what it takes to do the same job in a dramatically different environment.

Trust

The concept of trust has been thoroughly discussed in Chapter 1. If trust is absent or very low, participatory teamwork simply cannot work.

Shared Values

It is well established that values affect attitudes, attitudes affect behavior, and behavior affects job performance. The more employees work without close supervision, and the more they work with their brains instead of their hands, the more important it becomes for a team to operate with certain shared values. *Shared values* is popularly known as culture. Without shared values, employees with good intentions can go off in directions that are incompatible with organizational goals and objectives.

It is essential that you clearly understand why the unit exists—what its function or role is in the organization. Then you must determine what major beliefs, or core values, need to exist in every team member's mind to guide them in doing their jobs to achieve the goals and objectives that support the unit's role in the organization. Core values should be few in number and simply stated. In short, everything you do professionally should revolve around the establishment, maintenance, and perpetuation of those core values.

A distinct set of organizational values provides employees with a sense of identity and helps shape character, personal values, and behavior. Shared values affect performance in three major ways:

1. Managers give considerable attention to whatever matters are stressed in the value system.
2. Better decisions are made because team members are guided by their perception of the shared values.
3. Employees work a little harder because they are dedicated to the cause.

The Cornerstones of Teamwork

Successful teamwork is built on the cornerstones of leadership, talent, positive attitude, and interdependency. Consider these four elements when you develop a team.

1. *Leadership*. A team needs purpose and direction. Effective leaders create and maintain a cooperative team energized to fulfilling its purpose and accomplish its goals. Without good leadership, individuals in the group may, with good intentions, incorrectly focus their energy. Good leaders have a vision of what needs to be done and serve as a nucleus for getting others to work toward those goals.

2. *Talent*. Too often people say, "Hire the best people." Unfortunately, not everyone is the best. Since the very best people are scarce, it can be difficult to locate, attract, and keep them. Teams need people who are trustworthy and competent. The caliber of people needed on a team is a function of the goals and the pressure to get things done: The higher the goals and more intense the pressure, the more top people are needed.

A team that wants to be number one must have people who are among the very best at whatever they do. One way to accomplish this is to look at those people who are already doing well in their jobs and are good team players.

3. *Positive attitude.* Attitude affects behavior. Losers frequently use words like *impossible, can't, try, won't work* to express their feelings. These attitudes are self-defeating and self-fulfilling. On the other hand, winners frequently use words like *possible, it will be done, we are going to do it* to express their feelings. The old saying "Where there's a will, there's a way" is applicable to team action. And attitudes can be contagious. When the leader displays positive attitudes and results are achieved, the "can do" mentality becomes pervasive. It should be noted that *can do* does not mean "we cannot ever fail." Some caution and skepticism is both necessary and useful: It helps balance overoptimism. Only in the extremes is it that people get into trouble.

4. *Interdependency.* Some teams can function well with each member doing his or her own thing, however most teams require that people interact. As in any team sport, the group is only as good as its weakest player. When team members realize this, they are apt to strengthen or compensate for their weaker members. This does not mean that they continually carry them. Each member, at some point must meet minimum performance. But it does mean that people are more likely to be supportive when they realize they need each other to be successful.

No Prima Donnas

Teams can and will have individuals who are more talented than others. These people are often referred to as stars. Stars can be quite beneficial to team effort because they can serve as role models. However, stars cannot be allowed to exhibit an attitude that the rest of the team exists to support *them,* or that without them the team would fail. Stars are part of a "constellation" of team players. There may be many stars in one constellation. Stars on a team are very valuable as long as they do not feed their egos at others' expenses. When they do, they are a liability. They usually end up alienating the rest of the team. When this occurs, they cannot stay on the team.

The Framework for a Successful Team

Building teamwork that lasts is not a small undertaking. It requires determination, dedication, perseverance, and time. Teamwork develops incrementally, except possibly in a crisis, after which the team usually dissolves.

The guidelines in Chapter 3, in "Managing the Informal Social Structure," should be followed in consort with these additional guidelines.

Create an Operating Structure

All formal organizations eventually create some kind of structure to facilitate allocating responsibility, establishing reporting relationships, assigning functional roles, and dividing up work. Human beings are territorial creatures, and as such they make claims to territory. In organizations, territorializing may be in the form of space, responsibilities, money, information, equipment, or human resources. Once territory is acquired, it is not always voluntarily relinquished. Supervisors must remember that the most important reason for creating an organizational structure is to facilitate effectively and efficiently the achievement of goals and objectives. As a unit's functional purpose changes with corresponding changes in goals and objectives, changes in the unit's operating structure must be considered. In fact, whenever goals and objectives change, changes in the way the unit is structured most likely will need to be made. Depending upon how much flexibility is needed and how much autonomy employees will have determines how loosely or tightly structured the unit may be. Restructuring often involves redefining jobs, changing physical layout, revising standard operating procedures, and even changing work methods. This could necessitate retraining and cross training. Employee involvement in such activities is essential to assure success. When employees are involved in change, benefits are stressed, anxieties are minimized, training is provided, and adjustment time is factored into the equation, change will be more readily accepted. In changing structure and all else attendant to it, a certain amount of compromise and accommodation will be necessary.

Types of Teams

In deciding how best to achieve goals, a supervisor needs to consider the different types of teams that could be created. The following are examples of such teams:

1. Problem-solving teams. Based on the concept of quality circles, these usually consist of up to twelve employees drawn from different areas. They meet one to two hours a week to discuss ways of improving quality, efficiency, and the work environment. They have limited power to implement ideas.

2. Special-purpose teams. Usually evolving out of a problem-solving

team, these usually work on designing and introducing work reforms, integrating new technology, and meeting with suppliers and customers. These teams have major input into operational decisions.

3. Self-managed teams. Usually consisting of up to fifteen employees, these teams produce an entire subassembly, in some cases the entire product, or provide complete service. Team members learn all the tasks and rotate among jobs within the cell. The cell is a grouping of equipment and whatever else employees use to produce the product or provide the service. The team is largely self-supervisory and takes on many managerial responsibilities.

4. Project or task-force teams. Either very small or quite large, these teams consist of members drawn from other units and assigned for the duration of the project. The team has a very specific purpose, and when the purpose has been fulfilled the team disbands and members return to their home base.

Regardless of the type of team, however, it is best to involve all employees in the development of the team. Or, if there are just too many to make this practical, discussions can involve representatives of employees. For example, if restructuring to form a team will involve rearranging equipment, changing job classifications, and altering wage or salary ranges, employee involvement is requisite. Involving all potentially affected employees could be impractical; in such cases, employees chosen by some elective process would be essential.

Communicate Vision and Core Values

Supervisors must share their vision of what they are striving to achieve. They must also communicate their core values. Most important, they must be the embodiment and consummate role models of what they profess are their core values. If a core value is always meeting deadlines no matter how impossible, the supervisor must consistently meet deadlines, rarely failing to do so.

Involvement in Setting Unit Objectives

Team members should be directly involved in establishing unit objectives. Again, if the group is large, designated members should participate in goal setting. Goals should be few and realistically attainable. Too many goal-setting meetings results in the creation of too many ridiculously unattainable goals, or goals set for so far in the future that they approach fantasy.

Two or three goals to support the unit's prime directive may be quite sufficient. Every team member should be held responsible for having vision (an understanding) of what to do to ensure that the major goals are achieved. Team members also need to understand how what they will be doing requires support from others in the unit. There must be cross communication or employees will set out to achieve certain things that are in part dependent on some forms of assistance from others. If team members are unaware of what they will require from one another when assistance is not forthcoming, then because they are busy working toward their own goals, conflicts will occur and cooperation will be threatened. It is not unusual for goals to be modified once limits on how much team members can realistically assist others are known and understood.

Involvement in Developing Working Plans

Developing a basic plan of how goals will be achieved is an activity in which team members should participate. Since things rarely go according to plan, plans should not be overly detailed. It is often better to develop a basic outline and plan as you go. Supervisors need to remind themselves and all who report to them that the goal is to carry out plans and get results, and *not* to simply write plans. Too much time is wasted planning, and not enough time is spent getting things done. Too many people who spend countless hours planning end up seeing the goal of creating plans as the end result. Plans are not ends, but rather means to ends.

Involvement in Problem Solving

Team members do not need to be involved in every little problem that arises. However, when problems either cannot be readily resolved or many people are affected, it is useful to involve employees in problem solving. When employees accept responsibility for dealing with problems, they are likely to be less inclined to put the weight of the problems on supervisors' shoulders. When employees are involved in finding and implementing solutions, they are more likely to accept them and work at carrying them out.

Participation in Decision Making

Supervisors need to decide over which decision areas they want to retain exclusive authority. These areas should be communicated to employees either formally and/or informally. Supervisors also need to decide what decision areas they want to leave exclusively to employees. When employees have shared values and are trusted and competent, this area can be quite broad. Under such conditions, telling employees to use their own best judgement is a very good technique for building self-confidence and encouraging employees to take responsibility. All other decisions that fall somewhere between the two aforementioned areas should be open to employee participation. Employee involvement should be avoided if any of the following conditions are present:

- The supervisor's mind is already made up.
- Employees do not want to be involved in decision making.
- Employees lack the knowledge and/or experience to give meaningful input.
- Personal risk for employees far outweighs any potential benefits.

When employees are directly involved in decision making, it is essential the environment provide every employee with a relatively equal voice. Too often in participatory decision making a few voices dominate. Also, not everyone on a team is really equal; some people have more knowledge and/or influence than others. To create a level playing field, consider the following:

- When employees are brought together to resolve issues, present the issues and seek input to determine if they are correctly framed out.

- Ask each participant to write down his or her thoughts, suggestions, or solutions to deal with the issues. Suggest that no matter how off-the-wall their idea, they jot it down. Those "off-the-wall" ideas often trigger great ideas in other people's minds.

- Allow each person, one at a time, to present his or her ideas. A designated person should note down the ideas. Allow no discussion at this time, otherwise the more assertive members will accept or reject views, influencing others before they have a chance to speak. Avoid nonverbal communication like smiles, frowns, rolling eyes, and shrugs that might indicate approval or disapproval.

- After everyone has presented ideas, discuss them. If someone disagrees with an idea, challenge the idea, not the originator. Don't permit functional-role or other put-downs.

- After all the ideas are discussed, ask participants to silently rank the ideas. Collect the rankings and tally them: The idea that gets the most votes is the group's decision. Occasionally, so many ideas have been presented that no single one receives a majority vote. In such cases, drop the least popular ideas and discuss the remaining ones again. After re-discussion, vote. The idea with the most votes is the decision.

Participation in Reviewing Progress

At timely intervals, the team needs to take time away from doing and spend some time reviewing. If progress is not where it should be, then team members should participate in deciding what corrective action, if any, needs to be taken.

Stages of Team Building

Team building goes through stages of growth. When a new group is formed, whether all new employees, a mix of new and old, or comprised exclusively of seasoned veterans, the initial stage is the formative one. At this point members learn about each other, about their work, and about the environment. If the proper foundation has been laid, members will have positive feelings and want success. There will of course be some anxiety; after all, it is likely to be a new experience for most. It's a lot like marriage: Few people go into it wanting it to fail. There will be anxiety, but also a desire to see it succeed.

The Forming Stage

Members learn from the reactions of others what behaviors are acceptable or unacceptable to the group. They learn the ground rules for task requirements and interpersonal relationships. It must be remembered that each member brings his or her ways of thinking and acting, so there has to be some adapting, compromise, and accommodation.

Frictions and conflicts are not likely to be serious yet. Expectations, priorities, responsibilities, and standards of conduct have to evolve, be understood, and ultimately accepted. Some things will be set forth by the supervisor or higher management. However, if the team is to be highly autonomous or entirely self-managing, then the team itself determines much about how it will function. Obviously, whatever evolves must be acceptable to management.

If some team members are so mismatched that they will never fit in, they will leave on their own or are ultimately driven out by other team members. But if team members are fairly well matched, the chance of success far outweighs the possibility of failure.

The Storming Stage

As members begin to fit in and anxiety diminishes, they usually become more willing to speak up and speak out. Additionally, conflicts inevitably occur because people will occasionally get on each other's nerves. As people get to know one another better, some of what is learned will distress others.

In every organization there is an inevitable clash between people's need to retain their individuality and the organization's need for conformity. A team is a microcosm of an organization. Being a member of a team involves some loss of individuality in return for the benefits of being on the team. During this stage, group members can become antagonistic toward one another and/or the leader as their way of expressing individuality and resisting conformity. Covert and overt resistance to job requirements is most likely to occur.

The storming stage is the most difficult. If the team is unable to pass through this, or suffers severe damage, the team will ultimately fail. One way a supervisor can reduce conflict is to focus on each person's strengths. No one is perfect, and unless a person has serious flaws it is best to encourage acceptance.

Another way to avoid, minimize, or bring an end to serious conflict is to talk things out without pointing fingers. Ask embattled team members if they enjoy battling and want to see it continue, or whether they want to improve things. Stress common objectives and areas of agreement instead of disagreements. Also make clear the cost of serious conflict and the threat to job security. When causes can be identified, discuss realistic solutions to deal with them. When causes cannot be identified, develop and implement solutions that will change the situation.

Sometimes a crisis can bring about cooperation. If a crisis occurs, supervisors can use it as a catalyst for change. The threat of a crisis can also be effective. Occasionally, a third-party mediator will get people talking and cooperating. But the use of a counselor or mediator should be minimal, lest that person become a permanent part of the team. Ultimately, team members must be able to work out problems among themselves instead of relying on outside experts.

The Norming Stage

This third stage of teamwork development is when cohesiveness develops, new standards evolve, and new roles are adopted. Team members learn to be more trusting and supportive of each other. They learn to accept each other and capitalize on each other's skills. Best of all, they learn to work outside of their job descriptions and required roles, working together so all will benefit. For example, in the auto and steel industries, management and organized labor are, to varying degrees, in this stage. They have moved to this point after many years of conflict. Unfortunately, it took an economic crisis to trigger the realization that teamwork must occur.

The Performing Stage

In this last stage the team is fully matured and group energy focuses on achieving results. Accomplishing goals supersedes interpersonal rivalries and conflicts.

Teamwork is not a set of techniques per se. It is an operational philosophy about how to improve cooperation, commitment, and ultimately performance. As team members, supervisors can play influential roles in shaping teamwork. However, supervisors must bear in mind that in a climate of participatory teamwork, their roles are less than those of bosses and more of facilitators and coordinators. With responsible, trustworthy, and competent people, the participatory approach to teamwork will generate the best results over time.

5

Selecting and Assimilating Employees

In some organizations, supervisors still have little, if any, real input into the process of selecting employees. This practice is an organizational travesty. Human resources specialists, no matter how good their intentions, do not always have sufficient knowledge of the jobs for which they seek applicants. Supervisors do know these jobs and are in a better position to review applicants. While supervisors may not have as much training and experience in the selection process, they are in a better position to recognize if a person will fit the job and the organization, and be able to get along with other people.

The cost of recruiting, especially of highly knowledgeable and skilled employees, has risen sharply in recent years. There's a scarcity of people to fill many jobs. Considerable resources are wasted when the wrong person is hired for a job, or the right person is hired and placed in the wrong job. Also, it usually costs more to maintain new employees than the organization benefits from their services; after all, it takes time to learn how to do a job well in a new job environment. Poor personnel practices only lengthen the payback period.

When people are hired without proper screening and remain employed beyond an introductory, or what is commonly referred to as a probationary, period there's a higher probability of their becoming a problem employee. Whether represented by a union or protected by antidiscrimination legislation, most employees gain considerable job rights once they have completed their probationary period. It is difficult to discharge an unsatisfactory employee, particularly after the employee has accrued seniority or reached regular employee status.

The costs to organizations and to society of poor human resources practices are astronomical. Too often these costs are accepted as just another part of doing business, or else employers resign themselves to living with unsatisfactory employees. All supervisors recognize the long-term results of living with problem employees. Higher levels of management, who are to a degree insulated from day-to-day problems, are at times unsympathetic to the employee-relations problems of supervisors. After all, no problem is too big for the person who does not have to deal with it.

It is essential that supervisors formally participate in the selection, assimilation, and placement process. For an organization to do otherwise, it loses an opportunity for valuable input. The more people with different perspectives who participate in the selection process, the higher the probability that the correct selection will be made.

Even though many instruments and techniques are available to help evaluate potential employees, the interview process is still the technique that carries the greatest weight in the selection process. Unfortunately, even organizations that allow supervisors to participate in the selection process do not allow them to interview applicants. The arguments advanced are usually: "We can't afford to have the supervisor away from the work or the work area"; "It's too expensive"; "It's too time-consuming"; "They may ask questions that are illegal and get us into trouble." These defensive arguments are unacceptable when the costs of poor selection are considered. It's the classic case of being penny wise and dollar foolish.

The Selection Process

The selection process begins during the attraction phase. At this time, the requisites for the job are stipulated in the ads, the determination recruitment sources and the questions to be asked in the preliminary interviews are designed so as to screen out decidedly unqualified people. Next is the interview stage, then the hiring decision.

The interview is central to the selection process. The interview has always been essential, but it has become even more critical as an organization's use of reference checks, background investigations, pre-employment testing, and application information has been restricted because of protective legislation and changing social attitudes. In addition, applicants are becoming more skillful in the interview process. A skillfully planned interview can produce the appropriate job-related information needed to make an intelligent hiring decision. Key to effective interviewing is to understand its purpose: to gain a reasonably accurate impression of the applicant's qualifications and abilities. This information forms the basis for some of the crucial selection-process decisions that follow, including whether or not to extend an offer of employment, and if so, at what rate of compensation. The various activities that constitute the selection process are illustrated in Figure 4.

Who does what and when in each step of the selection process is influenced by such factors as the organization's size, its traditions and past practices, and the scope of responsibilities assigned to human resources personnel and/or supervisors. Naturally, the level of the job, the time constraints, and the competency and experience of people who interview and evaluate candidates play an important part, as well as the organization's current affirmative action goals and timetables.

The Selection Criteria

An interview cannot possibly succeed unless the interviewer has an understanding of the traits, characteristics, skills, training, and experience desired in the potental employee. Always remember that the primary goal of the selection process is to hire people likely to succeed in their jobs.

Study the jobs and employees in them who are under your supervision. People who do well in certain kinds of jobs often share traits and characteristics. Likewise, people who do not do well in certain jobs also have things in common. If you can identify certain factors as predictive of either success or failure, you will have a better idea of what to look for in applicants. Obviously, if an applicant exhibits the desired traits, then he is a viable candidate; if an applicant exhibits undesired traits, then he is not a viable candidate.

As simple as this sounds, it is often overlooked. Too often, those in the employment process do not have a clear understanding of what to look for in applicants for specific types of jobs in their organizational environment. Keep in mind that a person may have qualifications predictive of success in one type of work but of failure in another.

It is sometimes easier to pinpoint traits or characteristics that are undesirable than to identify to those that are desirable. While it is generally better to know the former, the latter are also helpful in the screening process. Even knowing only one trait helps screen out applicants. Of course, if

Figure 4. The selection process.

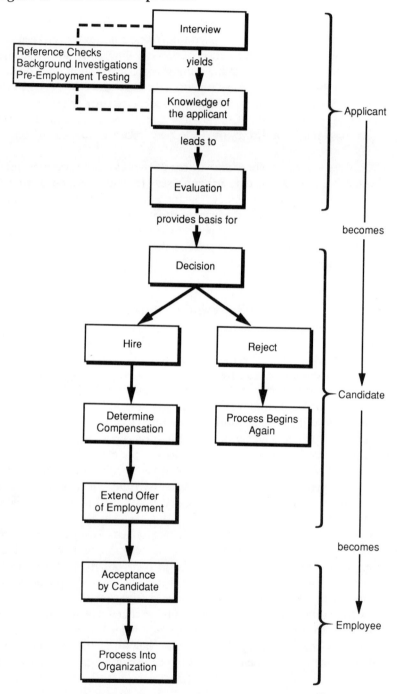

the job or work environment is substantially changing, the present desirable qualities may not be inappropriate. As jobs or job environments change, the criteria for success are also likely to change. In this case, you would have to assess the degree of change to determine your job criteria.

The Interview Process

Determining what information is needed and how to properly evaluate it to decide whether to hire or reject the applicant poses great difficulty for everyone. Interviews all too often fail to achieve their planned objectives and become little more than meaningless conversations. It is essential to thoroughly understand the traits, characteristics, education level, skills, and experience needed by qualified applicants so as to determine what information is needed and what questions to ask. Two simple guidelines can help in formulating questions: (1) They should be strictly job-related questions and (2) they should be nondiscriminatory. The extent to which you use reference checks, background investigations, pre-employment tests, and other screening tools then depends on how much information was gained in the interview.

Who conducts the interview, what kind of interview it is, and how many interviews there will be depends on the information needed. For entry-level and other lower-echelon jobs, interviews can be reasonably standardized. It is usually easy to ascertain whether an applicant has the requisite qualifications to be a word processor or machine operator.

These standardized interviews require little time. Most or all of the information needed to make a hiring decision can come from the initial interview, which should be conducted by human resources personnel. This is done not to exclude supervisors from the interview process but rather to relieve them of time-consuming initial screening. They can then refer successful applicants to the supervisors for further interviewing.

In certain situations—notably higher-level jobs, jobs requiring special skills or knowledge not readily assessed during an interview, or jobs requiring considerable team effort—an additional, effective interview tool is to have selected employees assist in the interview process. Their evaluation of the applicant can be a useful source of information and offers the added advantage of supporting management's hiring decision. It also can facilitate the assimilation of the newly hired employee into the organization at a later point.

There should always be overlap between the interviews by human resources personnel and those by supervisors. The degree of overlap usually depends on the job level. In positions on the word processor/machine operator level, human resources personnel can obtain most of the desired information. The job specifications for these jobs involve mostly routine skills such as typing or equipment operation, and whether or not an applicant has them can be readily discerned. In high-level jobs, where the tasks and duties are not so sharply defined and where such abstract skills and abilities as planning, directing, and reasoning are required, it is more difficult to determine the extent to which the applicant has these qualifications. Moreover, the risk and cost involved in making a wrong hiring decision increases with the job level. Therefore, at higher levels, the value of overlap between the interviews by human resources personnel, supervisors, and even employees is in sharing information and perceptions of the applicant's abilities and helping to either affirm or change initial and subsequent impressions. In addition, the degree of overlap is also influenced by the fact that supervisors and co-workers will usually interface more on a day-to-day basis with employees in higher-level jobs because of their shared activity and thus having a greater vested interest in knowing whom they are selecting.

The type of job involved determines whether the interview is conducted one-on-one, in a group setting, or a combination. Interviews for jobs involving extensive interfacing are sometimes conducted in group settings, where the applicant is subjected to group dynamics similar to what might be encountered on the job. Another advantage to group interviews is that several people can assess an applicant in one sitting. Group interviews require considerable planning and care to be successful. For instance, they can be threatening to the applicant, particularly if handled improperly.

Two interview approaches are most frequently used: directive or structured, and nondirective or unstructured. In a *structured interview,* the interviewer guides the conversation by asking the applicant specific questions formulated in advance. The advantage is that the interviewer can guarantee that all required information is obtained and unnecessary information is not solicited. The disadvantage is that the interview is too structured, and the interviewer tends to be more concerned with asking questions than listening to answers. In addition, structured interviews tend to cause anxiety for applicants, and they are apt to respond more to what they think the interviewer wants to hear than to say what they are really thinking.

The *nonstructured interview* involves open-ended and general questions so that the applicant may freely discuss likes and dislikes, needs, goals, experiences, feelings, and attitudes. This method attempts to find out how and what the applicant feels and thinks. Unstructured interviews are more difficult to conduct, since they require the interviewer to guide the conversation while being an effective listener. Interviewers must exert self-control and withhold their own ideas and feelings, and avoid expressing approval or disapproval even though an applicant may request it. This can be exasperating, but it is the way to obtain a more complete picture of the applicant. It is a difficult method to use effectively, requiring considerable training, so organizations often prefer supervisors to stick to a structured approach.

Effective results often come from a combined structured-unstructured interview. Interviewers solicit responses from a broad list of closed and open-ended questions, and allow applicants wide latitude in responding. When applicants stray beyond the question, interviewers guide them back. It is a good technique because it obtains responses to specific questions, but since the questions are not asked in a structured fashion, the applicant has latitude in responding. This reduces the applicant's anxiety and tension, while also requiring less skill and training on the part of the interviewer.

The Successful Interview

Training and advance preparation reduce the risk of failure in interviewing. It's important to establish an interview game plan. Determine in advance what general and specific information you need to make an intelligent decision about the applicant. Develop an itinerary if others are to participate in the process, and communicate the game plan and itinerary to them on a need-to-know basis.

Keeping in mind the job requirements, the law, and the applicant's right to privacy, as much information as possible should be secured and reviewed *before* the interview takes place. However, care must be exercised in not drawing too many conclusions about an applicant's character, experiences, skills, strengths, and weaknesses before an interview. In general, the more you know about an applicant before an interview, the easier it will be to establish rapport. Again, the danger in knowing too much in advance is that the applicant may be prejudged. Always remember, especially in interviewing, that first impressions spill over and often end as the final impressions. There is nothing ruder or more improper than reading over an applicant's profile, reference letters, or other material while the applicant is sitting in your office. This communicates that you really do not care about the person, otherwise you would have read the materials *before* the interview.

Keep in mind that the interview is an opportunity for mutual exploration. Unless a stress-type of interview is planned, do not add to what is already a stress-producing situation. Physical setting for an interview is just as important as mental setting. Before conducting the interview, establish the physical environment. Privacy and some degree of comfort are necessary for a good interviewing climate. Try to conduct the interview in a private area, and try to avoid any interruptions. If that is not possible, keep interruptions to a minimum. Hold off telephone calls and interruptions by bosses, peers, and employees unless they are emergencies. Frequent interruptions create about the same type of image as reading the applicant's record during the interview.

Have available nonconfidential information about the organization (its history, products, services) that the applicant will need to know or may inquire about. Anticipate the applicant's questions in advance of the interview; this will assist you in preparing your information base.

One of the first things the interviewer should do is put the applicant at ease. This can readily be accomplished by creating a somewhat informal atmosphere. Dress, use of titles, room setting, and seating arrangement can be used to create any range of climates. Offering a nonalcoholic beverage can help establish a good atmosphere. A firm handshake, clean appearance, articulate speech, and a direct look at the person are just as important for the interviewer as they are for the applicant.

Too many supervisors make the mistake of believing that interviewing is a one-way process and that the burden of proof is on the applicant. Many an applicant has turned down an offer, or has been turned off during an interview, because of receiving a poor impression. A brief introductory conversation about one of the applicant's hobbies or interests can start the person talking and establish rapport. Even talking about the weather can be helpful.

The less structured an interview, the more you need to know how to ask questions. Most poor selection decisions occur because interviewers either did not get enough information or did not ask for the right information. You should consider the following points when interviewing applicants:

- The more courteously a question is asked, the more likely an accurate or truthful response will be given.
- The first answer to a question is often a programmed answer. A follow-up question usually brings forth a more spontaneous answer.
- The word "why" is the most potent lie detector devised. Use of the "rolling why" (i.e., Why, why, why . . .) usually brings forth more information about an applicant.

- If information is positive, applicants will want to talk about it. If negative, they will not want to talk about it.
- There is probably no completely honest interview. When people give less than honest answers, their voice levels and volumes tend to drop. People rarely lie in a loud voice.
- What people like doing usually relates to areas of strengths. What people dislike doing generally relates to areas of weakness.
- Consistently late people usually have problems accepting authority.
- If an applicant gives a less than completely honest answer to a question, you need to assess its degree of seriousness. Significant lies are those by which an attempt is made to defraud. Such are grounds for immediate rejection. Insignificant lies are socially redeeming fibs that do not hurt anyone. Borderline lies are exaggerations. When an applicant significantly exaggerates something, it is important to find out what's behind it.
- Because applicants have been fired one time does not mean they are bad candidates.

Following are right and wrong ways to ask questions. Depending on criteria being assessed, you should choose a couple of questions from each category. The same specific questions need not necessarily be asked of each applicant for the same job, however the same question categories or topics should be. Remember, you get more information by asking open-ended questions.

Wrong (Closed-Ended)	*Right (Open-Ended)*
Do you feel you are qualified for this position?	How have your past job experiences prepared you, directly or indirectly, for this position?
Can you learn quickly under pressure?	Under what conditions do you feel you learn best?
Do you like people generally?	Describe what kind of people you like, do not like, and why?
How long have you been supporting yourself?	Under what circumstances, and at what age, did you become self-supporting?

Interview Considerations

In an interview, both parties must consider the short as well as the long run. You wonder, "Is this a person who can grow and make contributions to the organization?" The applicant wonders, "Is this a place where I can pursue my career?" Although we live in a highly mobile society, people and organizations often do establish long-term relationships.

You should become familiar with federal and state laws on equal opportunity and fair employment practices, and make certain that you do not ask questions that would be in violation of the law. In today's legal climate, information that is necessary to the selection process often cannot be obtained by specific questions. You must develop ways of asking pertinent questions indirectly. Human resources professionals are (or should be) knowledgeable about legal constraints and can provide supervisors with guidance and training in this area.

Take as much time as necessary to get your information about the applicant. This is especially true when the position is one of high responsibility and the wrong person can cost the organization a lot of money. In general, the higher the level of the position for which the applicant is being considered, the more time you should spend learning about him or her. The applicant should also have sufficient time to learn about the organization and the job(s) for which he or she is being considered. The worst thing that can happen to an organization or employee is to relocate the employee from another part of the country and then find out that a poor choice was made. It is advisable to give applicants who are being seriously considered a tour of the facilities and introduce them to some employees. Having other supervisors, higher-level management, human resources specialists, and some of the best employees interview the applicant is beneficial to all, since it gives everyone the opportunity to view one another from varying perspectives. Itineraries are important, although rigid time schedules should not be set.

Applicants should also be informed about the organization's current policies, practices, and compensation structure, including performance evaluation systems and procedures. Organizations tend to go to great lengths to put the best foot forward during the interview process. Applicants have a tendency to do the same. In the long term, it is better for all parties to be as honest as realistically possible.

Many organizations find it to everyone's benefit to interview the applicant's spouse. In dual-career families this is becoming increasingly important. A spouse who cannot pursue his or her career, or a spouse or children who have difficulty adapting to a new community, often cause problems for new employees. It is also advisable to arrange to dine with an applicant who looks promising. There is something equalizing about people eating together, and many communication barriers dissolve over a good meal.

In short, joining an organization is not that different from getting married. The more you find out about your spouse before you are married, the higher the probability that the marriage will last.

When interviewing an applicant, it is especially important to take *mental* notes. Some interviewers write down their impressions of an applicant while the person is speaking. Taking notes while interviewing will likely increase the applicant's anxiety and apprehension. The applicant might lose interest in the job in an attempt to figure out what is being written and whether or not a favorable impression is being made. Instead, take mental notes. When the interview is concluded and the applicant has left the room, write out your mental notes in detail, even if the applicant is not to be offered the job. Under present law, applicants who are turned down for jobs can file a complaint. The burden of proof for refusing to make a job offer rests with the organization. Written notes should be reviewed to finalize your impressions of the applicant. If many people are being interviewed for a position, you can review your various sets of notes later on to help you determine who is the best person for the position and why.

When an interview is completed, advise the applicant that either you or someone else from the organization will be in touch and how long it will take. Many organizations take much too long to follow up on an applicant, or do not follow up at all. Supervisors should also learn what constraints applicants are under in terms of needing a job or having other job offers. Of course, the date of the applicant's availability for work must be ascertained.

Dangers to Be Avoided in Interviewing

People have selective ways of interpreting what they hear. Like other people, supervisors have beliefs, feelings, and ideas about everyone else and the world. You must be careful to retain your objectivity when you interview. Some things that should be avoided in assessing an applicant are:

• *The so-called halo effect.* We have a tendency to identify with and relate to people who are like us physically, psychologically, and socially. To the extent that people are different, our preferences, biases, or prejudices often affect our objectivity. For example, a like or dislike for a particular minority may cause a supervisor to be consciously or unconsciously biased for or against an applicant from that minority group. At the same time, the supervisor must consider the extent to which group members will accept an applicant who is different from them. Obtaining employees who will fit into the organization and the unit and remaining in compliance with fair employment practices and equal opportunity laws may be difficult. As a supervisor, you are morally, ethically, and legally obligated to take some risks in hiring employees in order to be in compliance with the spirit and letter of the law.

• *Making generalizations from what has been seen or heard.* It's easy to overgeneralize from a statement the applicant made or from something you've observed. For example, you may conclude from an evasive answer that there is something unflattering in the applicant's background. Or the applicant may not be dressed in the latest style of clothing. Perhaps a personal contact did not give an unqualified endorsement of the applicant, or a letter of reference was totally honest in discussing the applicant's weakness and could prejudice judgments. There is some evidence to indicate that reference letters may not reflect an applicant's real qualities and qualifications.

On the other hand, because it is difficult to remove employees once they are employed beyond a defined introductory period, and the law often prevents asking some job-related questions, your conclusions must be drawn from the limited information you obtain in the interview. It is usually better, especially if you are experienced, to act on what you perceive if facts indicating otherwise do not exist. In other words, if you hear or see certain things about the applicant that arouse concern, it is better to be safe than sorry.

• *Hiring people who are significantly underqualified for a job.* If an employee, after training and reasonable time for adjustment, cannot be a contributing member of the group, problems will arise. This situation has been a real problem for organizations in instances where compliance with civil rights and related laws are concerned. The only viable way to avoid these problems is to not hire seriously underqualified people, or to establish meaningful remedial training programs prior to placement, followed by training on the job. I strongly endorse the latter. Organizations who maintain separate, lower standards of performance for underqualified employees do not benefit anyone, least of all the employees labeled as expected to perform less than up to everyone else's level.

• *Overcomparison with current employees.* While a new employee must fit into the work group, it is unrealistic to hire only people with similar social, economic, cultural, racial, or religious characteristics. Our nation is made up of people from many different backgrounds. The composition of an organization's work force should, considering the types of skills employed and labor market availability, reflect the composition of the community and the market served. The benefits of having a work force composed of people from differing backgrounds far exceeds the disadvantages.

The Hiring Decision

The hiring decision is the moment of truth. Hiring the wrong candidate can result in problems ranging from difficult to disastrous, and it can cost the organization untold sums of money, frustrate the supervisor, and especially important, result in the loss of a better candidate. At best, it is a process that involves risks. The objective is to reduce the risks through use of good decision-making techniques. Here are some practical guidelines:

1. Do not attempt to find the perfect candidate who possesses the education, skills, experience, and other qualifications that exactly fit the job specifications. Rarely, if ever, does that person exist.
2. Particularly in higher-level jobs, recognize that each candidate possesses certain unique talents and abilities that influence both the composition of the job and its contribution to the organization. In some instances it may be better to modify the job to fit the person.
3. The hiring process is one of compromise, particularly as it applies to higher-level jobs. Know where to compromise and how much.

In evaluating a candidate's education, skills, experience, and other qualifications, give consideration not only to how well the person meets the job requirements but also to how well the individual fills the future growth needs of the organization. For certain jobs offering limited growth, the candidate's potential may not be an important issue; and just as certain jobs are limited in what they can provide, not everyone desires to grow with the organization. But other jobs in more technical areas or in rapid growth environments demand that candidates possess additional potential beyond what is necessary to perform the present job.

Because of many economic and social influences, not every candidate will accept an offer of employment. A candidate's initial interest in the organization does not guarantee acceptance of a job offer. Just as the organization evaluates candidates, so do candidates evaluate organizations. Particularly in times of low unemployment, or when jobs involve much-needed specialized skills such as data processing or certain types of engineering, candidates are often highly selective.

Perhaps the most sensitive issue in the hiring decision is salary. Salary is frequently the major obstacle for both parties and is often why a candidate does not receive an offer or if received, the offer is rejected. Establishing a salary offer requires a delicate balance among what the candidate wants, what the market dictates the organization will have to pay, and how that salary will interface with the salaries of existing employees performing the same or similar kinds of work.

In establishing a salary offer, give consideration to flexibility. Depending on the organization's policy on salary negotiations, limits should be established. In lower-level jobs, especially when qualified candidates are readily available, there may be only a small range of negotiation. In higher-level jobs or in highly competitive market conditions, a greater range is usually necessary. Benefits and perquisites may also be negotiable in higher-level jobs, which tend to be more personalized and have more varied compensation packages. Particularly in the hiring decision there should be shared involvement and close cooperation between human resources and supervisors.

Extending the offer of employment philosophically involves considerably more than just offering a job with a certain salary and benefits. In one sense, offering a job is a mechanical function, but by itself it is incomplete. Granted, the job, salary, and benefits are important; beyond these, however, is the broader issue of offering a working relationship. During the interview process, an applicant usually gets a glimpse of the value an organization places on its employees. Whether that initial perception is valid, the actual strength of the organization's interest will be more significantly evidenced to the candidate by the offer of employment process.

In extending the offer of employment, then, an organization should demonstrate this interest through a discussion of its practices regarding education and training, career development, and generally those other activities designed to help employees realize their goals while increasing their value to the organization. By the same token, the organization should give consideration to the employee's potential to grow with the organization, depending on the job level. Studies show that a good job with a competitive salary and benefits is sometimes not enough to maintain the enthusiastic commitment of employees; these may be sufficient to attract candidates, but much more is required to elicit their enthusiasm and commitment. If employees feel that the organization places little value on them, problems ranging from employee unrest to high turnover are almost bound to occur.

Who makes the offer of employment is not nearly as important as how it is made. Generally, offers for lower-level job offers are made by a supervisor or higher-level manager together with the human resources personnel.

A simple phone call or face-to-face conversation is appropriate in lower-level jobs; in higher-level jobs, where the offer may involve agreements beyond the standard compensation package, it is advisable to make the offer face-to-face, with a follow-up letter outlining the agreement. In all instances, human resources personnel should provide counsel and guidance.

Assimilating the New Employee

This phase of the selection process facilitates the assimilation of the employee into the organization and, as required, into the community. While orientation is the mainstay of processing a new employee, there are other necessary activities depending on the job level and geographic relocation.

Orientation is frequently misunderstood and taken for granted. Employers spend vast sums of money and commit considerable time and effort in attracting, screening, and hiring candidates, yet often pay little attention to orienting once employees are on the job. No relationship can be taken for granted, particularly a business relationship that is highly dependent for its success on each party's understanding of its respective responsibilities and benefits. In fact, the effective utilization of employees actually begins with orientation.

Orientation is a time for the employee to become better acquainted with the organization, and the organization to get to know the employee. It is a continuation of the interview. Unlike the interview, however, the exchange of information now is aimed at cementing the new relationship and making it productive, mutually beneficial, and lasting. Since the organization already has considerable information on the employee, there is little immediate need for additional data except that required to process payroll and other information that was unavailable earlier because of privacy laws. On the other hand, employees are at a disadvantage. They often know relatively little about the organization, its products or services, its philosophy of operation, and where they fit in. Before they can truly become productive, they need to be given certain information.

Regardless of how educated, experienced, or mature new employees are, or of their job level, the transition to a new environment, even under the best of conditions, is anxiety producing. Unfortunately, there is little a new employee can do to reduce that anxiety. Clearly, the organization has to play the senior role in the developing relationship. It can provide the proper information, and it can take the appropriate measures to reduce the anxiety and ensure a positive experience.

Although the organization has these responsibilities, it has all too few initial opportunities in which to exercise them. First impressions made during orientation are long lasting and frequently correct. They are, moreover, difficult to change. Many organizations with high turnover can trace their difficulties to an ill-defined orientation process. The primary responsibility for orientation usually rests with human resources specialists. That is wrong. It should be with supervisors, with human resources specialists assisting.

Orientation is not a one-shot activity for new employees, and it should not be limited to reviewing a simple checklist of necessary information to be communicated. A complete orientation program could last six months to a year. It starts even before the employee reports for the first day of work.

When new hires or transfers are relocated, the organization and the supervisor should provide assistance with relocation. Anyone who has ever relocated has experienced the problems with finding housing, shopping, new schools, physicians and dentists, unfamiliar laws, and much more. Be in contact with a relocating employee before the first day of work. Allow the person time to get acclimated in the new community. Inform the people with whom a new employee will interface and encourage them to help the individual through the adjustment period.

Whether or not a formal orientation program exists, supervisors should be knowledgeable about their organization's history, products, services, philosophy, traditions, practices, standard operating procedures, opportunities, and benefits. To facilitate the flow of information, work from a checklist and have available all printed information about the organization. Just handing written material to new employees is insufficient; explain it to them.

Proper orientation is anything but informal. It should not be taken for granted. Its success, as ultimately measured in productive employees, is in direct proportion to the amount of planning and care it receives. In planning the orientation process, ask these questions:

- What general information does the employee need to function in the organization?
- What specific information does the employee need to perform a given job?
- Who will convey this information?
- Are the people who are assigned the responsibility for communicating the information trained for their task and are they effective?
- What are the sequence and timing for giving the information?
- Are there mechanisms to measure how much information the employee has received and whether he or she understands it?

- Are opportunities provided for the employee to ask questions and to give feedback?
- Is the overall effectiveness of the orientation process evaluated periodically and revised accordingly?

Certain items of information are basic to any orientation program, such as:

- Information about the organization, its background, its future, products manufactured or services offered, operating philosophy, comparison to similar organizations
- Information about the organizational unit to which the employee has been assigned, how it is vital to the rest of the organization, and procedures and rules germane to it
- Information about the specific job, special operating procedures, safety rules, and similar considerations
- General information such as selected human resources policies, pay practices, location of lunch rooms, infirmary facilities

The comprehensiveness and sophistication of the orientation process will vary with the organization's size and philosophy. In larger organizations, which have the benefit of highly specialized staffs and larger budgets, orientation typically is a formal, planned process. But this is not to say that small organizations cannot develop equally effective orientation programs. Effectiveness lies not so much in how sophisticated the techniques for presenting the information are but in how thorough and relevant the material is.

6

Improving Communication

Of the many problems that confront organizations and their managers, communication nearly always appears at or close to the top of any list. It is necessary for a leader to be able to effectively communicate with others. Supervisors may be knowledgeable, practical, or popular, but if they are ineffective communicators, they are apt to be unsuccessful.

Effective communication involves the transfer of information in ways that permit those who receive the information to interpret it and act upon it in the way intended. In other words, communication is the process of imparting ideas in ways that are understood by others.

Supervisors who fail to communicate effectively eventually lose touch with employees. To be effective, a supervisor must be able to sense the temperature and pulse of the employees, and sensing is accomplished by communication. Supervisors function in the role of a linchpin (see Figure 5), holding together the elements of the team. In the figure, the pin at the apex of each group represents the supervisor. Of course, in most organizations, people in one group are linked by formal and informal relationships with people in other groups. The more interaction that takes place, the more linking arrangements exist. The type of communication and the people involved define these linkup arrangements. The communication structures for these groups are dynamic because they continually change as formal and informal relationships change. Supervisors, in linchpin communication roles, have a considerable amount of information moving through them—from higher levels of the organization on down, from employees up to higher management, and horizontally through peer interaction.

If, as many are predicting, the trend to give employees more control over their work continues, the supervisor's communication role will quite

Figure 5. Linchpin communication systems.

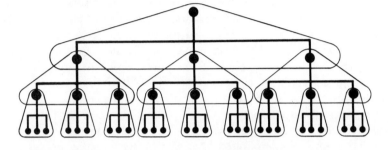

From *New Patterns of Management* by Rensis Likert. Copyright © 1961, McGraw-Hill Book Company. Used with permission.

Figure 6. Cellular communication system.

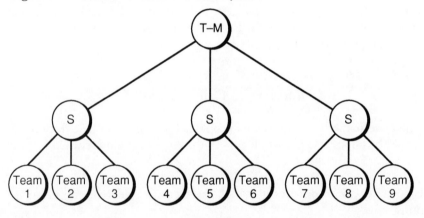

likely increase in importance. Because supervisors will have less direct involvement in what employees do on a day-to-day basis, they will have less opportunity to see with their own eyes what is going on. They will have to rely even more on communication to stay in touch with their employee teams. This means organizations will utilize a cellular communication system. Figure 6 shows such a system.

Most supervisors make a sincere effort to communicate with employees, peers, and bosses. They recognize that without the continuous movement of information, resultant problems will impede attaining objectives.

However, supervisors often become frustrated when communication processes do not work. To be an effective communicator, a supervisor must be an effective listener. Real communication occurs only when the receiver of the communication acts, or reacts, in the expected or desired way. *Real communication* means being sensitive to the needs and viewpoints of others, and objectively considering the receiver's point of view.

If your communication is to achieve its objective, it must be understandable. Everyone has moments of frustration when communicating with others, especially after thinking what was said was clear and straightforward. Why do misunderstandings or misinterpretations occur? Although communication is a complicated process, the facets of the process can be shown in a basic illustration. As Figure 7 shows, an idea is originated with the desire to communicate it to others. The originator of the idea encodes it into some communicable form, oral or written, and uses symbols, sounds, gestures, and expressions to directly or indirectly get the message to the intended recipient. By direct or indirect means, the recipient receives the communication, decodes it, and acts or reacts to it. The process of action or reaction is feedback. From the feedback, the sender is able to assess whether the communication was as desired.

Barriers to Communication

There are numerous reasons why people fail to communicate effectively. It would be impossible here to discuss all the types of communication barriers

Figure 7. Communication model (barriers to effective communication).

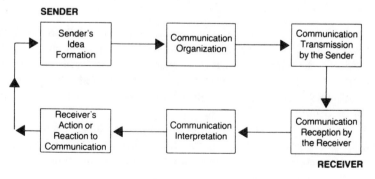

that exist, however the major sources of communication problems are identified and discussed. Consider to what extent these barriers are impeding your communications with people in your organization.

Sentiments

Each person views the world with biases, prejudices, values, feelings, attitudes, experiences, and beliefs—in a word, sentiments. Sentiments act as filters; each person interprets the world through a filter constructed of individuality and personal experience. For example, if you were to look at a green chalkboard, often referred to as a blackboard, and conclude that the board was black, it would be so in your eyes. After all, if it were green, wouldn't it be called a greenboard? Once you have arranged your "filters" to interpret green to be black, it would be difficult to convince you otherwise, regardless of how much someone tried to communicate that idea to you.

Language

Language may be spoken, visual, or written. Here, let's concentrate on spoken and written language. Even when people speak the same language, the meaning of words can vary widely. For example, government regulations and procedures, although employing the English language, are usually written in such a way as to confuse most readers. Figure 8 is an example of government's debased use of language.

Advertisements skillfully use words with multiple meanings to create certain images or impressions that may be accurate, partly accurate or totally inaccurate. The legal and medical professions are notorious for using the English language in ways that a person without training cannot understand.

In all your communications, employ the Imundo KISS principle, shown in Figure 9. Use simple words instead of complex words. Always think in terms of the receiver's ability to comprehend what you say or write. When people do not understand a word generally they do not look it up in a dictionary or ask for clarification. Most often, people either try to judge meaning from how the word is used, or else they just ignore the word and move on. If many words, especially key words, are not understood, the meaning of what you say is lost.

The longer your communication is, whether written or verbal, the more your meaning may get distorted or lost. Keep to the point unless there are compelling reasons to do otherwise. Complex communications should be

Figure 8. An example of government's debased use of language.

MAKING IT PERFECTLY CLEAR

The Federal Register's
horrible example of bureaucratese:

"We respectfully petition, request, and entreat that due and
adequate provision be made, this day and the date hereinafter
subscribed, for the satisfying of these petitioners' nutritional
requirements and for the organizing of such methods of allocation and distribution as may be deemed necessary and proper to
assure the reception by and for said petitioners of such quan-
tities of baked cereal products as shall, in the judgment of the
aforesaid petitioners, constitute a sufficient supply thereof."

—Federal government English

Translation: "Give us this day our daily bread."

—King James English

---

broken down into shorter, readily understood messages that are linked log-
ically.

Prejudice and Bias

Everyone has biases or prejudices. We tend to acquire them before adult-
hood, although throughout our lives we modify, drop, or reinforce these
prejudices. Words often trigger these prejudices because they carry associa-
tions. For example, *conservative, liberal, Old South, Jew, engineer, black, Irish-
man, Italian, senior citizen,* and *accountant* are words that communicate images
or ideas. When people classify and stereotype others, they tend to apply
their feelings and beliefs to all people who fall within the classification. Supervisors must understand the reasons underlying these prejudices and work
toward overcoming or controlling them. Prejudices are not easily concealed,

Figure 9. Imundo KISS principle.

K—Keep

I—It

S—Short and

S—Simple

---

and many people have developed a sensitivity (some would argue an over-sensitivity) toward identifying prejudice in others. Regardless, prejudices distort the message you send or the reaction you receive.

In addition to general prejudices, people have situational biases. A man may not have a general prejudice against women, but when a woman is in a position outside of what is perceived to be her normal role, prejudice may arise. This type of prejudice is sometimes exhibited toward women in top management or in other traditional male roles. The same could be said of men who keep house, cook, and shop for groceries. As everyone knows, we live in a changing world and we must be prepared to adapt. In other words, prejudice often outlives its acceptability and/or validity.

Position, Role, and Importance in an Organization

Organizations are environments of inequality. Authority, influence, title, function, compensation, and status are just a few of the ways by which people are differentiated. These differences become apparent when communication takes place. For example, differences in education level, background, title, uniform, even office decor often cause anxiety and apprehension in upward communication. It is not unusual for supervisors to feel some anxiety when they discuss something with the chief executive officer, especially in his or her office.

Differences in values are particularly evident in downward communications. For example, managers often think of change as a way to increase output, market position, revenue, or profits. Employees often interpret change to mean increased job responsibilities or changes in social position, security, or wages. While profits and wages are directly related, the average employee often does not fully understand this fundamental relationship. Therefore, communication should involve recognition of the receiver's values and be couched in language the person can understand.

Accurate upward communication is also difficult. Supervisors often view the information they give in terms of its possible effect on their power and prestige. Also, some higher-level people are not receptive to bad news. Rather than communicate bad news, supervisors communicate what the receiver wants to hear, or even nothing at all. All too well they recall the adage: If the messenger brings the bad news, kill the messenger. Also, they feel bad news may reflect unfavorably upon their own competency as managers.

Time

Timing of communication is very important. Anyone who has participated in negotiations or other sensitive matters has seen timing at work. When communication is timed improperly, the result is often not what was wanted. For example, suppose you want to ask your boss for a raise. After some deliberation, you decide that this is the day. You arrive at work, and when you enter your boss's office, she proceeds to inform you about various errors, losses, and other negative conditions related to your performance. You listen to her remarks and then, in accordance with your decision, you ask her for a raise. What are your chances of getting the raise? Not too good! The boss's frame of mind was such that a request for a raise would not be favorably received.

Sometimes delaying the sending of information is desirable. However, most often communications need to move rapidly so they can be received, analyzed, and acted upon. In business, failure to receive accurate information in a timely manner usually results in delayed and often poor decisions. The result of continued delays in information is failure.

Space

The use of space is very important in verbal communication. Space is the room we put between ourselves when we interact. In organizations, office space, desk size, seating arrangements, and decor all reflect a person's position and hence the amount of space he or she allows. Depending upon the type of information, structure, and parties to the communication, the space requirements we need can expand, contract, or remain the same.

People's space requirements are not always clearly defined. However, once the territorial circle is trespassed, reaction occurs and it may be either offensive or defensive. To illustrate, think about asking your boss for a raise when you are about one foot from his or her face. You certainly would infringe upon his or her territory, and your chances of getting a favorable decision are reduced. However, in a different situation and with a different person, communication in close proximity may be desirable. For example, two lovers merge their respective territories for intimate communication.

Supervisors must be sensitive to these communication barriers and work toward overcoming them. Following are additional barriers that may be encountered in your communications. These are of three classes: general, downward, and upward.

1. *General barriers*
   - Failing to understand personal motives
   - Showing unconcern or not giving feedback
   - Exhibiting feelings of self-righteousness
   - Perceiving one's superiority or inferiority
   - Protecting your prestige
   - Employing improper role playing
   - Being distracted by noise, lack of privacy
   - Having a hidden agenda or message
   - Lacking clarity in intent and meaning
   - Failing to express conviction
   - Showing poor listening habits
   - Telling half-truths

2. *Downward barriers* (Supervisor to employee)
   - Intimidating employees
   - Not finding time to listen
   - Lacking concern for employees' values or interests
   - Showing weak leadership
   - Being untrustworthy
   - Talking down to employees

3. *Upward barriers* (Employee to supervisor, supervisor to higher management)
   - Being suspicious, fearful, mistrustful
   - Lacking confidence
   - Being prejudicial against people in power
   - Limiting yourself to your own value system
   - Using improper language

Understanding the Channels for Communication

Supervisors, in their relationships with others, must carefully examine all facets of the communication process. These include the environment, the situation, and the persons involved. Most communication problems stem from problems in relationships. Problem-solving approaches such as writing more effectively or learning how to give a speech, while useful, rarely get to the underlying cause. To get at the core of the problem, you need to understand the nature of your relationship to the person with whom you are communicating. Communications in business generally move through two identifiable channels: the formal or network, and the informal, commonly known as the grapevine.

Formal Communication Channels

Formal communication channels are established by formal relationships, job descriptions, tasks assignments, methods and practices, technology, laws, and procedures. These channels parallel the formal lines of authority and responsibility, identified in organizational charts, policy manuals, and standard operating procedures.

In most organizations, formal communication channels become set in concrete. Since power and status are associated with initiating, distributing, and receiving communications, it is easy to understand why so much emotion surrounds an organization's information system. It is also easy to understand why there is often great reluctance to change the established flow—changes in flow usually cause changes in power. This is why, in some organizations, personal computer workstations and computer networks have not been exactly embraced by all. Under the cloak of propriety of information they have attempted, albeit without success, to maintain control by centralizing information and controlling its movement.

When you feel it is necessary, question the validity and reliability of information communicated through the established channels. The movement of information must facilitate the accomplishment of objectives. As objectives or approaches change, the systems that generate and distribute information must also change. Unnecessary and improper movement of information wastes time, energy, talent, and money. In today's fast-changing world, managers at all levels must continually ask whether information they receive or generate helps or impedes getting things done. Computers are excellent tools for creating, analyzing, communicating, and storing information. However, far too often electronically generated information survives longer than its intended purpose, or in some cases never really serves a useful purpose. If you are receiving unnecessary and/or the wrong information, inform those who create it. Get yourself out of the information distribution channels that do not provide useful information. Unfortunately, organizations are awash in useless and/or irrelevant information.

Remember, the less time you have to spend handling useless or unnecessary information, the more time you can devote to using good information. Useful information facilitates better communication and improved decision making.

Some of the questions that you must ask when analyzing communications and the channels through which they move are:

- How valid and reliable is the information?
- What results are actually achieved with this information?
- To what degree is this information necessary for accomplishing the objectives?
- What are the true costs of generating and distributing this information?
- Who was involved in generating the information? Who is involved in its distribution? What are these people's motives?
- Is it necessary for these people to continue generating or distributing the information?
- If this information is necessary, can the costs of generating and redistributing it be reduced? How much?

When changing any facet of a communication process, remember that organizational politics is involved. Needless to say, considerable skill is required to change a system without generating an avalanche of problems. Most supervisors lack the authority to change formal organization communication channels. However, you can point out to those who have authority the reasons why change needs to take place. This may involve personal risk, but then, effective supervisors are prudent risk takers.

In using formal channels of communication, supervisors tend to place heaviest emphasis on the downward flow of information, communicating with employees. Downward communication helps to bring the different levels of an organization together. Unfortunately, not enough emphasis is placed on developing good channels of upward communication as well. Effective upward communication starts at the bottom of the organization and moves up through each level to the top. As a supervisor you should create an environment whereby employees feel free to communicate their feelings and concerns, as well as accomplishments and activities, to you. You need this feedback to determine if what you have said to employees has been received, properly understood, and will be complied with to the degree expected.

In general, downward communication serves to initiate the feedback process; it is mostly of an informative or directive nature. The resultant upward communication tends to be more of a questioning and reporting nature, including giving suggestions, concerns, and complaints. Compared to the roar generated by downward communication, upward communication is a whisper. In creating the proper environment for upward communication, you must show that you want the straight facts about employee feelings and concerns; though difficult, you want a climate free of risk.

When we speak of upward communication, of course, we are dealing with different levels of power and status in the organization. Even under the best conditions, it may be difficult for employees to be totally candid with the people who impact their jobs, salary, or work assignments. Nevertheless, remember that if employees do not have channels within the organization through which they can communicate their feelings and concerns, these feelings and concerns will find other outlets. The results are usually undesirable. When negative feelings are expressed through family, friends, and other social interactions, the organization's image suffers. Today, as never before, good employees are hard to find. No organization wants to be the employer of last resort. In addition, society allows an organization the privilege of serving. When society perceives that the disadvantages of an organization's operational behavior exceed the benefits, it will, through competition or government regulation, take what it believes to be corrective action.

When upward communication does not work, the results also are often costly. When employee feelings are not expressed at all, they build to a critical mass, and may result in an explosive emotional reaction such as sabotage, a walkout, a lawsuit, civil action, or unionization attempt. The key to avoiding these problems is to develop appropriate channels through which frustrations and anxieties can be constructively addressed.

In addition to formal downward and upward communication in an organization, there is a horizontal channel of communication. The horizontal channel may also be multidirectional, depending on the organization's structure and the dynamics of the informal channels. The flow of lateral information is essential when there is a high degree of interrelatedness and interdependency.

Informal Channels, or Grapevines

Many supervisors fear grapevines and try to control or eliminate them. Eliminating the informal communication system is not only undesirable but absolutely impossible. If one channel is destroyed, another will quickly be established. This is because of the nature of people, relationships, and the need for information. Effective supervisors learn to cultivate grapevines and use them to benefit the organization, its employees, and themselves.

Develop an ear for grapevine communications—it will help give you insight into what employees are thinking. Information moving through the grapevine tends to be partly correct; distortions occur only because of personal interpretations and rumors. Grapevines go around and cut across formal organizational lines to communicate information very quickly. They tend to be most active when employees are apprehensive, anxious, frustrated, tense, or insecure because of actual or expected changes within the organization.

Because of unstable social relationships, grapevines have no explicitly defined pattern or duration. Participation in grapevines varies according to the formal structure, the informal social structure, the nature of the people who have access to the information, the people who are affected by the information, and other variables. People who tend to be very active in grapevine communication are those who either have, or are aspiring to, social position or popularity.

One of the dangers of grapevine systems is the distortion: from distortion, rumors often arise. You can minimize distortion by following a few simple rules. First, establish a relationship of trust and confidence with employees. Employees must see you as a person who will give straight answers to questions, or reasons why answers cannot be given. Second, never lie to employees. If you do, take corrective action by confessing to the lie and then being honest in the future. An admitted mistake is more likely to be forgiven; a covered-up mistake that is later uncovered usually is not forgiven. Third, anticipate what types of information cause concern among employees. By explaining the meaning of certain changes before distorted meanings are generated, you can minimize problems. When employees are not given reasons for changes, they develop their own.

In any organization, there are people who attempt to increase their influence, or information power. They often do this at the expense of the authority, prestige, and influence of supervisors. Some employees find it to their advantage to cultivate or embellish rumors, especially when it increases their prestige among peers. This readily results in a power confrontation. Supervisors who have established relationships of trust and confidence with employees, and especially with the informal group leaders, will be able to easily deal with employees who try to gain politically at their expense. All the supervisor has to do is tell employees that what they have heard is not correct, and that the person who has told them this information has distorted the facts or lied. Employees will then discredit the rumor starter. On the other hand, a supervisor who is not held in high regard by employees is limited in discrediting rumors. In some instances, mistrusted supervisors who attempt to discredit a rumor may find their efforts turned against them by the rumor starters.

Supervisors can manage the grapevine system in another way, too. They can use the grapevine to communicate information that they do not wish to communicate formally. For example, you might recognize that formal discipline of an employee would generate the wrong results. You could use the grapevine to inform the employee that his or her performance is not up to expectations and that if change does not occur, formal action will be taken. Peers often have more latitude in saying things to one another than supervisors have.

Meetings

Meetings can be forums for communication or big wasters of time. Unfortunately, too many meetings end up as the latter. Obviously, you have more influence in a meeting you call or conduct, as compared to those you are required to attend. Assess what occurs in a meeting and what results afterward. If meetings need improvement, identify the changes necessary.

Some of the factors that make for ineffective meetings are:

• *Lacking purpose.* The scheduled meeting has become institutionalized; in effect, it is ritual whose original purpose either has been long forgotten or whose need passed years ago. Everyone wonders why he or she is there, but no one has the courage to openly question why there is a meeting.

• *Sparring session.* Some meetings are nothing more than institutionalized forums for disputes. Everyone comes to watch the fight(s). When heavyweights are going to fight, it usually attracts a larger audience.

• *Too casual.* Some meetings are comparable to a open house: People come late and leave early. Agendas are derailed and such meetings are characterized by distraction and confusion.

• *No focus.* Some meetings have a merry-go-round agenda. Too many issues are discussed while real issues are avoided. There is a tendency to table issues or create task forces and subcommittees. The meeting gets bogged down in irrelevant debates, speeches, and commentary. Issues are discussed, but are rarely brought to closure and no actual decisions are made.

• *Process taking precedence.* Some meetings are conducted with more concern for process than for results. They are conducted in strict conformance with procedures and rules, while all meaningful debate and discussion is stifled.

• *Game playing.* Some meetings are characterized by inordinate amounts of gamesmanship, or show and tell. Each participant has to tell what he or she accomplished, each embellishing what was accomplished so as not to be outdone by others. Others play games of beating one's breast by telling how hard he or she suffered for the organization.

Your meetings can be more productive by employing the following ideas:

• Determine whether a meeting is really necessary. There may be a much more efficient and effective way to accomplish what you want.

• Limit who should attend. The more people who participate, the less likely attendees will have an opportunity to be actively involved. Unless communication is primarily one-way—the leader talks while participants listen—when lots of people attend, splintering of groups is more likely to occur.

• Unless there is good reason not to, tell participants in advance about the purpose and agenda of a scheduled meeting, with sufficient notice to allow participants to adequately prepare for the meeting.

• Consider the timing of a meeting. Meetings scheduled an hour or two before lunch or quitting time will likely drag on until lunch or quitting time. Friday afternoon meetings that continue long after quitting time will only anger participants. On the other hand, a 4:00 P.M. meeting when 5:00 P.M. is quitting time could motivate participants to make progress. A breakfast meeting or meeting over lunch may offer more advantages than a meeting during normal work time. The timing for a meeting is a matter of judgment.

• Set a schedule. In deciding what to include on a meeting agenda, develop a rough idea of how much time it will take to cover each agenda item. Occasionally, an major issue should be broken down into more manageable tasks. Making progress toward a goal is critical for maintaining interest in and enthusiasm for meetings.

• If important, tell participants in advance to be prepared to discuss what is on the agenda. Again, agendas should normally be distributed in advance.

• Meetings, unless for extraordinary reasons, should always start on time. It is rude and disrespectful to those who are there to wait for latecomers. If the boss is habitually late, talk privately with him or her and point out the costs incurred for waiting.

• Unless an emergency arises, meetings should not be interrupted. Lock the doors to the meeting room. Ask participants to shut off beepers, pagers, alarm watches, and never permit portable telephones in a meeting. If there is a telephone in the meeting room, disconnect it. Allow no messengers to make deliveries.

• Avoid hidden agendas. They create a climate of distrust.

• As necessary, influence the debate, dialogue, and discussion. Praise the contributions of participants. Avoid knocking people down in public unless absolutely necessary.

• Try to avoid letting a discussion become too rhetorical. Move discussions to closure; focus on getting results, not on the process itself. Assess your progress and review the results.

• Before going on to new business, decide if it is better to finish old business first. Also, consider allowing time for nonagenda items.

Vocabulary and Delivery

Since most communication in organizations requires both written and spoken language, choice of words is important. The English language is very complex, with words often having multiple meanings. In addition, different words mean the same thing. Because of their backgrounds, experiences, values, and the like, people attach different meanings to words.

Because language must be receiver oriented, using words that people do not understand usually causes them to turn off. Most people are reluctant to use a dictionary or ask for clarification; nobody likes to display ignorance. And this is true throughout all levels of organizations. On the contrary, overly simple language often causes receivers to perceive the communications as condescending. The key is to use plain English that will be easily and readily understood. Occasional use of words not readily understood is acceptable if the receiver can easily figure out what is meant by context in which it is used.

When the speaker can be observed, body language is also important to communication. Appearance, posture, eye contact, facial expressions, arm waving, finger pointing, foot stomping, and the like either enhance or detract from communication. People who are successful at influencing others know how to put their whole personality into communication. Their body movements and speech complement one another.

As part of effective oral communication, vocal quality is important. Pitch, tone, articulation, volume, and rate of speech all influence your spoken messages. Speaking too softly or too loudly may be irritating and distracting to receivers.

Determining Feedback

When a message is communicated, feedback is obtained. Remember, what is communicated must lead to action. People must react to communication.

There are two techniques for obtaining and assessing feedback. First, ask the person to whom the communication was directed to repeat the message and what it means to him or her. If the listener can repeat the message with the proper interpretation, it is safe to conclude that it was understood. Understanding, of course, does not mean that the expected or desired action will occur. Second, judge the listener's behavior after the message was received. Body movements, facial expressions, changes in posture, and eye movements all provide nonverbal feedback. This form of feedback can be observed only in face-to-face communication.

Listening

Being a good communicator also means being a good listener. Supervisors need to listen accurately to the information or feedback they receive. Good listeners actively listen on three levels at all times: They hear sounds and voices, they grasp the meaning and implication of the words, and they absorb and process the information. A good listener attempts to get the feel of what is being conveyed—not just part of it, but the whole of it.

Good listening habits can be developed by following a few simple rules:

- Some speakers are not very articulate and therefore have difficulty expressing their thoughts and feelings. Others are long-winded and take what seems to be forever to make their point. Good listeners learn to be patient. Impatient listeners may motivate speakers to stop communicating.
- It is difficult to keep listening to a message while disagreeing with its content. Even if you disagree, continue to listen so you can properly assess the message. Prejudgment, or impulsive judgment, is detrimental to good listening.
- Some speakers display annoying mannerisms or project a negative image. Good listeners do not let prejudice or bias effect their receiving and interpreting of communications.
- When people do not understand the message being sent, they usually stop listening rather than ask for clarification. A good listener asks for clarification of what is not understood.
- Some people would rather talk than listen. A good listener waits until the message sender is finished before replying.

Communications With the Boss

Supervisors can increase their own authority by influencing their own supervisors. However, far too often they either do not try to, or do not know how to influence their bosses. To influence people, you need to understand their value system. People have a tendency to reject communication that is contrary to their values and accept what is in consonance. Therefore, being able to "read" the boss is important.

In profit-driven organizations, the prime value of higher-level managers is profits—the bottom line. When communication is phrased in terms of how money can be saved or made, it is better received. Where organizational survival is, for all intents and purposes, guaranteed, concern for employees may far surpass concern for profits. Regardless of what conditions exist, supervisors need to understand the higher-level manager's value system and communicate within those values. For example, suppose a supervisor wanted to spend some money on sending selected employees to a training program. Outright asking for the money, especially when money is tight, is likely to be met with a negative answer. However, opening with words that speak to making or saving money, explaining how and when such will result, and then asking for training dollars is likely to increase the likelihood of a positive answer.

Supervisors must also recognize that most higher-level managers are not formally disposed to hearing phrases like "It's impossible," "It cannot be done," or "I'll try." Likewise, they don't want to hear that you need more time, money, equipment, or people; that the project will not be on schedule, or that you will overrun your budget. Higher-level managers are more favorably disposed to hearing phrases like "Consider it done!" "We are underbudget," or "We are ahead of schedule."

Some supervisors have a propensity for dumping problems onto their boss's lap. They go into their boss's office and say "We have a problem." A smart manager is likely to respond "We have no problem, only you do because I do not want to hear about it." Supervisors need also to recognize that some managers like to hear suggested solutions to problems while others prefer to create solutions. Again, the key is understanding the manager's basic thought processes and value system.

Another thing to understand is that while bosses generally do not like to hear about problems, they hate surprises even more. Decide what problems can be resolved without your boss's knowing, and which ones have to be brought to his or her attention.

Often times, when a supervisor suggests something to the boss, it is met with a negative response. Many higher-level managers like to test a supervisor's convictions, willingness to persevere, and initiative. Learn to interpret when a negative response really means no, and when it means "try again." Initiative, conviction, and perseverance are desirable qualities in managers at all levels. Just as important is a supervisor's knowing when to back off and abandon or temporarily shelve an idea.

Most higher-level managers are very busy people. Recognize that, while it appears the boss never seems to have sufficient time for you, the time allocated is probably more than he or she should make available. Have your thoughts organized and make efficient use of the time allotted. Also, remember that higher-level managers who have a number of supervisors reporting to them are not always fully knowledgeable about where each is and what each is trying to accomplish. Therefore, inform your boss, or bring him or her up to date, before you make your request.

Communications With Employees

Supervisors, by virtue of their role as leader, are often privy to more information about the organization than employees. Sometimes information is of a sensitive or confidential nature. Employees to varying degrees are curious about the effect decisions made by others will have on them. Though it is important for employees to feel they belong to the organization, no organization can be completely open with its employees about all its operations. Leaks of confidential or sensitive information can have adverse consequences. What information should be communicated by supervisors to employees? Following are examples of information that employees usually need or want to know, without risking security:

- The history of the organization, its products or services, and how the products or services are developed and marketed. Most employees know little of what their organization does and how it operates.
- Organizational policies and procedures that affect employees.
- Major organizational plans for change and how employees will be affected. This information must be properly timed. Too much information too soon could be just as disastrous as too little too late.
- The ways in which employees' jobs fit into the organization's operations.
- The organization's system of promotion, wage increases, and other rewards.
- The organization's rules, regulations, and disciplinary action system.
- How employees can get a hearing for their complaints or grievances.
- The organization's future in terms of its short- and long-range objectives. The prospects for steady employment and opportunities for advancement.
- The organization's general financial condition. The disclosure of profits, however, must be tempered because many employees may not understand the concept of return on investment or the need to invest in new equipment to maintain competitive advantage.
- Information about layoffs, if they should become necessary—the reasons as well as the possible duration.

This list is not all-inclusive, but it can be helpful in planning and organizing your communications with employees. Develop your own list of what you think employees should know.

7

Providing Leadership

Whenever people work together toward the accomplishment of a common objective, an organization comes into existence. Some person or group emerges to direct and coordinate the activities of others for the purpose of accomplishing that objective.

If leadership is absent or ineffective, members of an organization will behave in ways that cause problems that eventually lead to chaos. When leadership is present and effective, the activities of others are defined and carried out so that objectives are achieved with a minimum of problems. Leadership positions, or roles, exist in organizations because they are necessary. In the long term, leaders remain effective only if followers are willing to cooperate. Cooperation may be achieved by force or it may come about voluntarily, but it is usually preferable to secure cooperation by voluntary means.

Whether or not leadership is effective involves the complex interrelationships of leaders, followers, internal and external environments, and many other circumstances and conditions. Some of these factors are laws, the state of the economy, the organization's position in its business(es), its financial condition, philosophy, traditions and practices, technology, capitalization, size and structure, and customers.

Management literature contains rich and diverse information about every conceivable aspect of leadership. I will not elaborate upon these research findings here. Instead, I discuss leadership from broader perspectives with the objective of helping supervisors understand the concept of leadership and how to use this knowledge to assess their own effectiveness. Supervisors, by objectively assessing the results of their leadership methods, can then determine if change is required to increase their effectiveness.

Broadly speaking, leadership techniques—or what are often called styles—range from highly *directive,* or authoritarian, to highly *nondirective,* or participative. An example of authoritarian style is a supervisor's ordering an employee to do something without giving the employee any right or opportunity to question the order. An example of a participative approach is a supervisor's discussing various courses of action with employees and allowing them to participate in making a decision, or in making the decision entirely on their own.

Many writers persist in what is really a futile attempt to convince managers at all levels that business organizations can be managed in a democratic fashion, where everyone has an equal voice in making decisions. While the trend is toward more involvement in decision making, it is unrealistic to believe that business organizations, particularly those employing large numbers of people, could be run on a one-person one-vote basis. The delayering and downsizing of organizations, and the concurrent emphasis on employee empowerment, has led to more democracy in the work place. However, there are many reasons why employees cannot and should not be involved in all facets of decision making. Consider the following:

- Sometimes decisions have to be made quickly in order to capitalize on an opportunity or avoid or resolve a problem.
- Employees do not always have the necessary knowledge to contribute in meaningful ways.
- Some decisions need confidentiality because of their sensitivity.
- There are decision areas where employees have little if any interest and would rather not be involved.

With knowledgeable, responsible, competent, trusted employees, supervisors can and should encourage involvement in decision making. However, encouragement is one thing and willingness to be involved is another. Employee willingness to participate is directly related to need, interest, and perceived rewards versus costs.

Leaders as Discriminators

Most organizations today experience fundamental problems in exercising authority because many people still believe that everyone should have the same rights, privileges, authorities, and compensation as everyone else. This general belief is known as *egalitarianism,* and it is incompatible with a healthy capitalistic system. In terms of economic and political philosophy, it is socialism. People may profess that everyone should be treated the same, but in reality they want to be treated as individuals. To prove the point, try this simple experiment. Hire two people and assign them to different tasks. Put one in a very strenuous, demanding assignment and the other in an easy one. At the end of a specified time period, pay both people the same wages. What will the reaction be? Obviously, the person who performed the more demanding activity will perceive that he or she has been discriminated against and has been taken advantage of.

Inherently, people do not want to be treated the same as others; they want to be treated fairly and according to merit. The bases upon which people are treated differently, and the ways in which they are differentiated from one another, have concerned people from the beginning of time. Since people want to be treated differently, managers at all levels must discriminate; discrimination is implicit in the concept of leadership. Failure to discriminate creates instant mediocrity: Those who deserve more are inadequately rewarded and those who deserve less are overrewarded. The challenge to all leaders is to discriminate on a basis that is legitimate, ethical, and moral, and to do it in ways that others perceive as fair. Only when people perceive that the advantages of everyone's being treated the same are greater than the disadvantages will they opt for the same treatment for all. As discussed in Chapter 3, supervisors must continually find ways to treat people differently and do it in ways that are fair. Fairness is an elusive concept; it will be discussed in Chapter 8.

Evolution of Leadership Methods or Styles

If we examine the leadership methods, or styles, practiced by managers in free societies over the last 100 to 150 years, a gradual overall shift in methods can be observed. Keep in mind that this is a generalization to which there are many exceptions. The methods or styles have shifted from highly directive, or authoritarian, to more nondirective, or participative.

There appears to be considerable misunderstanding about what participative management is. It does not mean that supervisors and employees have equal voice in decision making, as some are inclined to believe. In a participatively managed group, employees have meaningful input to the decision-making process, but the final decision most often rests with the supervisor. The supervisor retains veto power over the recommendation of employees because the supervisor is the person who has the final responsibility for the accomplishment of objectives. To use this approach effectively, supervisors must be willing to listen to and consider employee input to decision making.

Styles of leadership in general have shifted over the years for a number of reasons. Many people in leadership positions still have not accepted the idea that today they cannot lead people in the same ways they did in the past. Indeed, most leaders have sort of backed into less authoritarian approaches to managing. Leadership involves the exercise of power, which many people enjoy; the right and ability to exercise power is one of the attractions to leadership positions. This does not mean that all leaders are power hungry and eager to dominate others. It does mean that a lot of satisfaction can be derived from exercising power, especially if it is used to benefit rather than harm.

In recent years a considerable amount of research and resultant literature have attempted to convince people that nondirective, or participative, styles are the best for all concerned. But this view is often incorrect. Many things influence the effectiveness or ineffectiveness of leaders and the styles they develop and apply.

The gradual shift in applied leadership styles has been caused by the interrelationships of many factors, events, circumstances, and conditions. Broadly speaking, leadership styles have shifted from highly to less directive because of:

- Changing social values
- Laws protecting workers' rights (civil rights laws, labor-management relations laws, work environment laws, and fair employment practices laws)
- Supply and demand in the labor market
- Competition, domestic and foreign
- Declining profit margins
- Unions and their countervailing power
- Higher levels of formal education of workers
- Higher levels of formal education of management
- Increasing costs owing to scarcity, higher taxes, and other factors
- Evolution of the global work place, where employees and facilities are distributed around the world, thus making it difficult to manage from one central location
- The growth of volunteer employees who work in organizations because they want to and do not have to (related to the aging population and increased number of retirees)

It appears that for the foreseeable future, these factors continue to influence the leadership styles practiced by all levels of management.

Changing Attitudes in the Work Place

It is common knowledge that employees today have values and attitudes different from those of employees of a generation ago. Because change happens so fast, generation gaps—different values and attitudes—are probably wider today than in the past. Supervisors cannot live in the past or long for the past when employees were easier to manage. They must recognize what presently exists and adapt to it. When employees' values are considerably different from those of supervisors, there is the potential for (and likelihood of) conflict. When there is a lot of conflict, in the near term, supervisors may have to force their decisions on employees, accept the increased costs of control, compromise and adapt within limits, or capitulate and, in effect, abandon their roles and responsibilities. The long-term solution to employee attitude problems is to educate employees to understand that they can satisfy their needs by cooperating to accomplish organizational goals. It is only a healthy capitalistic system that is able to provide jobs, pay income taxes, and support social programs.

Many employees need to understand that they cannot always "do their thing" in organizations. Privileges or freedoms are earned by demonstrating responsible behavior. This process of education (or re-education) is not an easy task.

Government acts and reacts according to input from society. A democratic government, if it is to survive, must remain popular: It must be responsive to society's needs. Society's input into government decision making is often contradictory. Often, one group pushes for one thing and another pushes for the opposite. Because a large portion of society has, sometimes for valid reasons, become suspicious of organizations (in particular businesses), government has enacted and vigorously applied a plethora of laws, regulations, procedures, directives, and rules affecting organizations' functioning. Many of these laws have increased the costs of doing business, restricted decision making, and created artificial demands for employees with special training such as human resources specialists, lawyers, and accountants. Some recently enacted laws are popularly referred to as "lawyers' full employment laws." Complying with federal, state, and local laws has been so frustrating and confusing for all levels of management that they have sometimes lost sight of the reasons for the organization's existence. Employees have also developed a certain sophistication in calling upon the administrators of the law for protection or justice and unfortunately sometimes just to hassle employers.

Supervisors must understand the basic reasons these laws have been enacted and become knowledgeable as to how they impact their roles as leaders. Supervisors must also recognize that they cannot and will not be supported by higher-level management when they operate outside the spirit and letter of the law. Supervisors are more likely to violate employment relations laws out of ignorance rather than intent. This is why it has become necessary for supervisors to consult with higher-level management, human resources, and/or lawyers when making potentially sensitive decisions about employees.

For many reasons, we have seen wide variance in the supply-and-demand factors in the labor market. Technology, population shifts, nonadaptive educational systems, lack of human resources planning, changes in the law, and changing consumer preferences are some of the factors affecting the supply and demand for labor. When certain skilled people are in short supply (for example: certain types of engineers, nurses, plumbers, accountants, electricians, or physicians), what is known as a seller's market is created. The people who possess the skills that are in short supply and for which there is high demand have their choice of employers. If they become dissatisfied because of the way they are treated, they can and often do quickly change employers. Loyalty to organizations is a thing of the past. Supervisors must be sensitive to this condition in directing all employees, particularly employees whose skills are in short supply.

Declining profit margins, rising costs, competition, government regulations, and management complacency have served to point out that all levels of management, especially the supervisory level, must lead employees in ways that create or help to create climates where employees want to make a strong commitment toward achieving organizational goals. People, if managed properly, can be an organization's most valuable asset. As global competition intensifies, it will take increasingly better leadership in organizations to enable America to successfully compete.

Countless arguments about the benefits and liabilities of unions have been put forth for many years. Unions are a powerful influence in most democratic societies. They are a part of America's institutional structure. In unionized organizations, supervisors must learn to work cooperatively with union leaders to help make the union's presence an asset. One real benefit of a union's presence in an organization is that it will force managers at all levels to be better, or pay the price of ineffectiveness in costly grievance settlements, arbitration, and restrictive labor-management agreements. In nonunion organizations, supervisors must recognize why people join unions and, if it is within the scope of their authority, not create incentives for employees to seek union representation.

An interesting dichotomy exists in America. It is estimated that approximately 25 percent of the adult population is functionally illiterate. However, a large percentage of today's employees have completed high school and gone on to advanced training in colleges, universities, vocational and technical schools. While the quality of their education can be debated, awareness and expectations have changed. In his book *The New Realities* (New York: Harper & Row, 1989), Peter F. Drucker has referred to these employees as knowledge workers. They have less loyalty to organizations, increased awareness of opportunities open to them, more mobility than their predecessors, and have made increased demands on other employees. Managers at all levels must lead in ways that meet these kinds of employees and others expectations. Problems occur when employees' expectations exceed, in large measure, an organization's abilities to meet them. Supervisors must also educate employees to understand the practical limits of what organizations can make available to them and why these limits exist.

It is apparent that the highly autocratic approaches to managing that were so commonplace a hundred years ago, to a degree are no longer useful. In the short term, the authoritarian approach is highly effective, however in the long term it often produces negative results. Theoretically, the participative approach is better. However, does the theory work? That is a complex question because many factors affect the success or failure of a general leadership style. For instance:

• The technical structure of some jobs gives employees less flexibility in their work activities. Some jobs in factories and offices are so structured by technology that the work must be processed only in one way. In these cases, participative management generally is not very applicable.

• Some jobs are potentially so dangerous that no deviation from standard operating procedures can be permitted. Therefore, participative management cannot be practiced except on a very limited basis.

• Some organizations, such as the railroads, government, and trucking, are so highly regulated that participative management's applicability is somewhat limited.

• Participative management can work only if employees are willing to assume responsibility. In many organizations, management does not want employee input in decision making, nor do employees want to participate in decision making. Within reason, employees will comply with directions issued by others.

• Unless high trust and confidence exist, participative management will not work. If higher management refuses to support employee input, it will be difficult to put it into practice.

• The organization's reward system must be geared to risk taking and goal accomplishment, and its discipline system must be geared to correcting the behavior of those who do not perform up to standard or expectations.

Acquiring Leadership Authority and Responsibility

Authority is the legitimate use of power. It is sanctioned by society or organizations and their members. Authority carries with it a concurrent responsibility to use it properly. As the cliché has it, "abuse or misuse it, and you lose it." Power, in contrast to authority, requires no formal sanctioning or legitimacy. For example, suppose you meet a man in a dark alley who points a gun at your head and threatens to shoot you if you do not give him your money. Would you refuse and argue that he has no right to ask this of you? Of course not. While he has no legitimate right to rob you, he is able to influence your behavior because the gun in his hand gives him the power. Of course, you always have the choice of not complying, however the probable cost is getting shot and possibly killed. The cost is usually sufficiently high to make most people comply.

Most applications of authority are accepted. When employees feel, for any reason, that authority is exceeded, they covertly and overtly seek ways to question and even resist that authority. This is the use of countervailing power. Supervisors must always remember that they retain their authority only so long as its legitimate use is approved, and its application is accepted over time by the majority of those who are supervised.

Authority is usually vested in an individual, or the opportunity to develop it is sanctioned, by an organizational process. Authority is a dynamic process that is affected to varying degrees by many factors. For example, as people, situations, or relationships change, authority changes. Authority is conferred (although it is rarely defined exactly as something one can or cannot do) by any one or combination of the following.

Function

The importance to the organization of the job and employees supervised is the *function*. Such importance shifts with changes in objectives or operational constraints. In recent years, product-design groups, quality-assurance groups, and financial-control groups have become more important and as a result more politically influential.

Position

The person's formal rank within the organization is the *position*. Job titles and their meanings vary considerably among organizations. The title of president implies a different level of power from that of supervisor. Titles like group leader, superintendent, director, chief executive officer, chief engineer, dean, chairman, and manager all connote some degree of authority. Position titles should be correlated to the relative level of power to facilitate employee understanding. For example, to most people the title Chief Executive Officer implies a higher organizational position and concurrent degree of power than the title Assistant Manager. If the reverse were true, it would confuse many people.

Knowledge

There is an old saying that knowledge is power. People who have knowledge that is useful to the organization can share or withhold their knowledge as a way of asserting power. Supervisors must be somewhat knowledgeable of the work they manage. In some instances, such as with working supervisors, they may be the most technically knowledgeable members of their group. However, high levels of technical knowledge are maintained at the expense of managerial skills. Today, it is rather common for some employees in a unit to have more technical knowledge than supervisors.

Supervisors must recognize the power of the knowledge that employees possess. Dissatisfied employees who possess necessary job-related knowledge can, and often do, find ways of withholding knowledge to restrict cooperation when so motivated.

Personality

People in positions of authority sometimes possess and exhibit charisma. People inherit certain of their traits and characteristics and develop others.

How we look, feel, believe, think, act, and react all change, to varying degrees, over time. Based on their perceptions, people continually assess the benefits and liabilities of relationships. The higher the degree of attraction employees have to their supervisor, the more the supervisor is able to influence their behavior. In effect, supervisors are able to increase or extend their power because their traits and characteristics are perceived positively by employees. Of course, the opposite conditions could exist. Power based on charisma is quite fragile because people's feelings, beliefs, and attitudes can change quickly. Supervisors can use their charismatic authority to supplement other sources of authority. It is risky, however, to use charisma as a substitute for regular bases of authority.

Additional Factors

Other factors affecting the development of a person's scope of authority include the number of people supervised, the worth of equipment under control, the size of budget, the political support from superiors, and various situational factors.

Authority: Acceptance and Resistance

Every supervisor at one time or another has observed that some employees will do almost anything they are asked to, promptly and without complaining. In addition, whatever they are asked to do will be done well. These are the employees supervisors dream about. In some organizations these employees are few in number, while in others they are plentiful. Most supervisors, at one time or another, also have employees who do as little as possible and complain at every opportunity. When they finally do what they have been asked to do, they often do an average or less than satisfactory job. These two extremes have been shown for illustrative purposes. Everyone has observed, in different situations and under varying circumstances, behavior ranging within the two extremes.

Why is it that some employees always seem to be fighting back? Why do some employees always cooperate? There is no simple answer. Background, experience, values, situational variables, perceptions, diet, attitudes, beliefs, feelings, and even heredity all influence behavior. However, the process of employee acceptance or rejection can be discussed in a general way.

Every person has within him or herself what can be identified as a zone of acceptance of authority. This zone is dynamic, and its size is influenced by all the factors mentioned above. Figure 10 illustrates the concept of zones for two people. Employee A has a wide zone of acceptance while employee B has a narrow zone. The zones illustrated for these employees can be for a given situation, or can represent an average zone observed over an extended period of time.

In the situation illustrated, employee A will accept, without some form of resistance, more direction than employee B. The shaded area shown in (b) illustrates the difference in the direction that will be accepted by A and B. Any supervisor would prefer to have employee A rather than employee B in his or her unit. Supervisors should avoid hiring employees who have narrow acceptance zones. Unfortunately, as discussed in Chapter 5, supervisors often either have little, if any, voice in the selection process. In addition, zones of acceptance do not remain static; many factors cause the zones to either expand or contract.

The objective is to develop within employees zones that are wide. This can be done by force—that is, fear, intimidation, harassment, or cajolement—but this approach requires that the pressure be constantly maintained. As soon as the pressure is reduced, or employees develop stronger opposing forces, the zones will shrink again. When employees voluntarily widen their zones, no pressure is necessary; supervisors need only maintain conditions that motivate employees to maintain wide zones. On the other hand, some supervisors erroneously believe they should have employees with

Figure 10. Zones of acceptance and resistance (for two people).

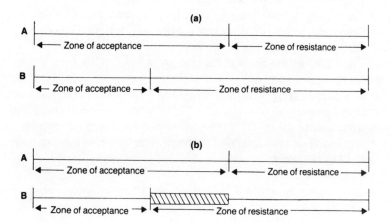

zones that are as wide as possible. But the problem with employees who accept everything without question is that a supervisor does not get the feedback necessary to influence decision making.

Resistance to authority can show itself in many forms, but whenever employees frequently resist authority, supervisors ultimately lose. A supervisor may be able to outsmart or outmaneuver some of these employees some of the time, but he or she can never outsmart or outmaneuver all of them all the time. Employees have the advantages of time and, if many are involved, numbers. Besides, tremendous resources are wasted when supervisors and employees conflict. Think of what could be accomplished if the antiorganizational creativity displayed by some employees could be channeled into cooperation and productivity. Employees motivated to resist and retaliate may spend the better part of their workday, and even time outside of working hours, thinking of ways to restrict, resist, and retaliate.

Following are just a few of the almost infinite ways in which employees can resist authority:

- They forget to do something after being asked and hope that the supervisor also forgets. If caught, they use defenses such as being too busy or not having enough time.
- They comply to the barest minimum possible, also known as marginal compliance. Next time, the supervisor might ask someone else to do it.
- They argue strongly that it is someone else's turn. They claim harassment and discrimination if the supervisor persists.
- After being directed to do something, they go to the supervisor every few minutes and ask how to proceed to the next step.
- They complain of illness and needing to seek medical treatment.
- They take a day off from work when all employees know they will be badly needed.
- They fake an injury or claim that an old injury has been aggravated by doing the job.
- If a grievance procedure exists, they file a lot of grievances over a short period and take considerable time to write or discuss them.
- They overtly or covertly sabotage equipment or misfile paperwork.
- They steal or conveniently lose something that is needed to maintain the flow of work.
- They spread rumors.
- They make accusations of racism bigotry, prejudice, victimization, and the like.

- They complain that it is not their turn and that they are being singled out for discrimination and/or persecution.
- When asked to do something, they contend that it is not in their job description.
- They make frequent trips to the bathroom.
- They give dirty looks, are disrespectful, and do other things to keep the supervisor on edge.
- They complain about everything and anything.
- They refuse to comply with directions.

The only really effective way to deal with resistance is to identify the underlying cause of such behavior and develop plans for corrective action.

In any organization, group dynamics exist. Formal and informal groups, in addition to individuals, develop zones of acceptance of authority. The degree of difference that may exist among the zones of the organization, supervisors, employees, and the employees' friends or peer groups is important to understand. Figure 11 illustrates a zone for the organization, the supervisor, an employee, and the employee's peers. Each zone differs in width. In this example, the organization has the widest zone of acceptance. (Keep in mind that an infinite number of combinations could exist.) The zones decrease in size down to the employee, who has the narrowest zone. As shown in the figure, if the organization issues some directive at point A, the supervisor accepts it without question, since it is within the supervisor's zone of acceptance. Since the directive is also within the zones of the employee and peers, acceptance and compliance will occur.

Figure 11. Zones of acceptance and resistance (for the supervisor, the organization, an employee, and the employee's peers).

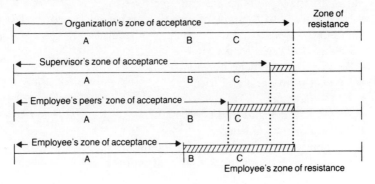

Problems will start to occur when the directive issued by the organization, the supervisor, or both shifts to point B, as shown in the figure. In this case, the directive is within the zones of the organization and the supervisor, however it is outside the acceptance zone of the employee. The employee will be strongly motivated to resist, but will not be supported by peers because the authority is within their zones of acceptance.

If the directive is at point C, the employee will be motivated to resist strongly and will be supported by peers because the authority is outside of their zone of acceptance as well. This situation will inevitably result in a confrontation between management and employees. Either management influences employees to widen their zones to accept the directive, or the resistance of employees motivates management to shift the decision back toward point A or B.

The model in Figure 11 can also be drawn to show the effects of the upward movement of information. In these instances, information emanates from an employee or the group, and would be accepted as legitimate or illegitimate depending upon where it fell in the supervisor's and organization's zones. The ideal organizational environment, and one that should be the goal of all organizations, is for the zones of the four factors (employee, peers, supervisors, organization) to match as closely as possible. When this occurs, and if the zones are wide, the highest possible levels of cooperation exist.

Zones of acceptance are affected by many variables, some of which are listed below.

- Understanding the nature of the directions employees are asked to accept.
- Perception of consistency or inconsistency of the directions with regard to employee purposes and objectives.
- Experience with the type of direction. What happened the last time employees were asked to do something similar.
- Perceived rewards for acceptance.
- Perceived punishments for noncompliance.
- Support from peers and friends.
- Self-confidence.
- Supply and demand in the job market.
- Physical or mental health.
- Credibility of the person issuing the direction.
- Sense of professionalism and level of training.

It is important to remember that the interrelationships of these factors, and the weighting of them, vary greatly among people and according to general and situational influences.

What It Takes to Be a Leader

Is there such at thing as a natural leader? People are not born leaders. They may have inherited or developed traits and characteristics that motivate others to identify and be influenced by them, but this is a function of prevailing values and norms, which often change. Considerable research over the years has led to the conclusion that people who exhibit certain traits and characteristics are more likely to succeed as leaders over the long term. The traits and characteristics of effective leaders are interrelated with the skills required for effective supervision, as outlined in Chapter 1, however a number of traits can be correlated directly with leaders. These correlations can be made whether the leaders are presidents and supervisors, or informal group leaders without title or sanction.

Effective leaders generally have a better vision of the future. They can see opportunities where others see emptiness. Steve Jobs, one of Apple Computer's founders, envisioned the personal computer market long before competitors saw the opportunities. Effective leaders also have the ability to recognize talent in people and get ordinary people to do extraordinary things. They know how to judge people, events, and situations. They can often inspire people by effectively relating to them.

People who become leaders tend to have a stronger drive or greater perseverance. In the face of adversity, they persevere to reach their goal. Anyone who takes risks faces the possibility of failure, but when failures occur leaders are able to analyze and learn from the failure and renew their effort to reach a goal.

Effective leaders are skillful in communicating. They are able to identify with and relate to those with whom they interact. They are skillful in applying verbal and nonverbal techniques to influence others. They understand human behavior and how to influence it. They are able to create conditions or situations where people's needs are met by following the leader.

Another characteristic of leaders is that they tend to display high achievement drives. High achievers not only compete against the standards of others, they develop their own standards. In a sense, their need to achieve can be satisfied only for short periods of time. High achievers are continually looking for new opportunities and challenges. These people may be very creative and bring success to themselves, to others with whom they interact, and to the organization. They can be an organization's most valuable assets, however they can also be an organization's worst liability. High achievers may exploit organizations and employees for the sake of personal gain. High achievers may also fail to recognize that they are different from other people and that other people may not be able to move at the speed and intensity that they move. This could lead to employees either withdrawing or rebelling.

Competent leaders display a high level of social and psychological maturity. This means that they not only know what to say and do, but how to say and do it. They have also developed an acute sense of timing; that is, they know when to say and do something. Many people have developed the skill to analyze problems and develop and implement solutions, but unless they know the right time to implement the solutions, they will not solve problems. Supervisors who have had to negotiate, especially with union leaders in labor-management talks or grievance negotiations, learn to develop a sense of timing or they become ineffective.

Leaders display an ability to absorb and retain knowledge that is greater than that of their employees, and they usually are more intelligent. Intelligence and intellectual capacity, to a degree, are measurable, although standard IQ tests alone are insufficient. Intelligence is, in part, inherited. Intellectual development, however, is largely dependent upon stimulation, conditioning, practice, and reinforcement. Owing to inheritance factors, one person may have a higher level of intelligence and even the capacity to learn more than others. However, if that intellect is not developed through stimulation and conditioning, its potential will not be realized. On the other hand, with proper stimulation, conditioning, practice, and reinforcement a person born with a lower level of intelligence could conceivably develop to a much higher level than the person who started with more.

Historically, societies have had a love-hate relationship with people who are more intelligent than the masses. Leaders at any level often find themselves simultaneously admired and respected, feared and despised. Leaders must be sensitive to the degree to which their intelligence arouses jealousy and fear among others. It is well understood that the more inferior and threatened a person feels in the presence of someone else, the more he or she will try to avoid that person. If avoidance is difficult or impossible, nonviolent or even violent means may be used to remove the threat. Leaders should not hide their intelligence, but they should be aware of how they display it.

Effective leaders have the self-confidence that allows them to take risks and accept responsibilities. Faceless bureaucrats, in both industry and government, tend to be risk avoiders and therefore avoid responsibility. As the sign on the desk of former president Harry Truman read, THE BUCK STOPS HERE. Leaders, if they are to move forward, must be willing to assume risk and accept responsibility for success or failure.

Self-confidence is an important factor in a leader's willingness to make decisions. Decision making and responsibility go hand in hand. Leaders are the people who have to make key decisions. They must be able to absorb information, assess courses of action, weigh the risks, make the decisions, and assume the responsibility.

Leaders generally know how to conduct themselves when interacting with others. This does not mean a high level of social etiquette, although it does not hurt to have it. It does mean being able to control one's emotions without being unemotional. Joy, affection, tenderness, anger, resentment, and jealousy are all human emotions, and if they are not displayed, serious psychological problems may arise for supervisors and people with whom they have contact. The critical factor is knowing when, and to what degree, to display these normal emotions and feelings.

Another facet of effective leadership that is only recently getting attention in universities and management literature is moral courage and integrity. Leaders must have the courage to make difficult decisions despite their unpopularity. They must also have a high level of moral integrity and set an example for others to instill a sense of moral integrity in them.

Leaders, particularly business and political leaders, must be able to function at a high level of moral integrity within the complex web of different cultures standards and values, and the interrelationships of personal, religious, organizational, societal values, and prevailing laws. They must also be able to predict and adapt to changes occurring in society. In the modern world, such is a very significant challenge.

Developing an Effective Leadership Approach or Style

As leaders, supervisors develop and employ various approaches to directing the activities of others. You may learn how to lead by following the examples of predecessors or other leaders, or may develop your approach by trial and error. Observation, training, evaluation, and trial and error interact to shape your approach to leading and serve as feedback in developing the approaches or styles that work over the long term. There is no "best" approach because the effectiveness of any style is a function of three general interrelated variables: the traits, characteristics, and needs of leaders; the traits, characteristics, and needs of followers; and a broad range of environmental and situational variables.

Some people enjoy controlling the activities of others, but the degree to which they have a need to control varies widely. People are, to varying degrees, attracted to leadership roles in structured organizations such as the military, or paramilitary organizations like police and fire-fighting units, because the structure, symbolism, rituals, and uniforms satisfy their need to lead in a directive or authoritarian manner.

People with different personalities and temperaments are attracted to leadership roles in organizations such as some universities, think tanks, and research laboratories because the comparatively loose structure, informality, and less rigidly defined roles satisfy their need to lead in a less directive, more collegial, or participative manner. Because leaders have different traits, characteristics, personalities, and temperaments, their needs to lead in various ways vary widely. To be effective, leaders must be reasonably well matched to the environments where the approaches or styles with which they are most comfortable will work to bring about positive results.

Leadership styles in organizations are affected by a broad range of environmental and situational factors, of which the following are some examples.

- The leadership style exhibited by supervisors, up to chief executive officer. (In some organizations leadership styles depend on the length of the shadow cast by the person in the top position.)
- The degree of control of decision making structured by organizational procedures, regulations, and rules.
- The presence of a union and negotiated labor-management agreement.
- The level of danger present in the work place.
- The financial condition of the organization.
- The organization's position in its industry.
- The process of determining budget.
- The supervisor's degree of responsibility and accountability.
- The way in which work is scheduled.
- Prevailing values, norms, attitudes, traditions, and past practices.
- Legal constraints.
- Technological constraints.
- The degree of quality required in producing products or services.

- The size of the work group or team.
- The kind of behavior rewarded by the organization.

Leadership is too complex a process to be considered just a function of a few variables. For this reason it is impossible to say conclusively that a particular style of leadership should be practiced by supervisors. What works for supervisors in one organization could bring disastrous results if applied in another organization. Leadership styles must be designed and tailored to fit.

Delegation

No manager likes to feel he or she has lost control. Supervisors are ultimately responsible for the performance of units under their direction or guidance. Yet when authority is given to employees, supervisors have relinquished some degree of control. Some supervisors have no problem sharing authority with employees, while for many reasons, some have great difficulty. It's likely no supervisor has the time or skills to do all the work personally. Supervisors almost always have to rely on the cooperation of employees, but if control over employees is too tight, it is likely to restrict them in getting things done. On the other hand, if control is too loose, some employees may, out of ignorance or intent, behave irresponsibly. The dilemma every supervisor faces is what and how much should be delegated. There are no precise answers to such questions. There are only considerations to guide you in answering these and other questions relating to sharing authority. While the overall trend in management is to give more authority to employees, delegating must be approached with some caution lest control be lost. The following considerations should prove to be helpful in understanding more about the process of delegation, the hazards, and the benefits.

For many years supervisors have been told they could delegate authority but not responsibility. This notion is only partly correct. While supervisors are ultimately responsible for the performance of the units they supervise, employees can be held accountable and indeed responsible for what they do or do not do. In effect, when employees are assigned to tasks and given the authority to do what is required, they can and should be held responsible for the outcome.

The degree and extent to which delegation of authority, responsibility, and tasks does or does not occur has a far-reaching effect on what occurs in organizations. When control is highly centralized, employees do not learn to handle authority, make independent decisions, or grow to be self-reliant and self-sufficient. They also often fail to develop new skills or even expand their existing skills. They often end up as semiskilled emotional eunuchs. Employees have opportunities to grow and develop only when authority and responsibility are accorded to them.

The extent and degree to which delegation occurs impacts on organizational efficiency. Overdelegation leads to a loss of control while underdelegation leads to inefficiencies if the decision maker is not on top of everything all the time. Delegation also affects employee stress. Too much work without the ability to handle it can overwhelm employees. Too little work when the desire to have more is present can be very frustrating.

As mentioned earlier, some supervisors can readily delegate whereas others cannot. Some of the factors affecting a supervisor's delegation patterns are the following:

- Supervisor's degree of personal security. Insecure supervisors have considerable difficulty delegating because they fear either losing control or looking bad if employees do things better than they.
- Supervisors may be constrained by technology, higher authority, safety, or law from delegating much.
- Supervisors may suffer from perfectionism—"if you want it done right, do it yourself."
- Supervisors may believe, or with certainty know, that employees are not trustworthy and/or competent.
- Supervisors, especially those who have to live with excessively high turnover, may feel rightfully so that they do not have the time, nor is it worth the effort to train employees to do things they can easily do themselves.

To guide supervisors in determining what should or should not be delegated, the following thoughts are offered:

- Have a clear understanding of the unit's prime directive, its primary function or role in the organization.

- Recognize the constraints, be they technological, organizational, financial, or legal, that limit what you can and cannot delegate.

- Clearly understand the essence of your role and just what you get paid for. Focus your time and energy on the essential, critical aspects of your job.

• If you are a perfectionist, consider the law of comparative economic advantage: If you make $30 an hour (wages and benefits) and an employee makes $10 an hour (wages and benefits), who should do the task if it can be done in one hour by you and two hours by the employee?

• Determine what decisions you want to maintain proprietary control over, then consider what decisions to involve employees in, and last, what decisions should be turned over in entirety to employees.

• Recognize and accept the fact that if you died tomorrow, the world would still continue to function.

• Recognize that unless employees are given opportunities to learn, they will never grow and develop.

• Recognize that if you wish to be promoted, you had best have a suitable replacement ready to fill your position.

• Keep in mind that you are paid to manage and not to do the work that employees are paid to do.

• Unless you are a working supervisor, avoid getting directly involved in employees' work. Exceptions are if you are training, an emergency condition exists, or you have nothing else to do and employees could use a helping hand.

• Remember that the more accessible you are, the more available you become, and the more tempted you may be to check in with employees to see how things are going. "Staying in touch" is a euphemism for staying in control. Consider not always leaving a telephone number where you can be reached, not always carrying a portable telephone, beeper, or pager. Over-accessability can cause overdependence.

• When you give authority and responsibility to employees, establish checkback and feedback requirements. It is also important for employees to know where they can go for lateral guidance and assistance.

Leadership provides guidance and a sense of direction for employees. Effective leadership often motivates ordinary people to become extraordinary. While there are many approaches to leading, the best ways are the ones that bring about positive results over time. It is also important to remember that actions always speak louder than words, and you should lead by example.

8

Effective Employee Discipline

Discipline is essential to all organized group action. The members of any organization must control their individual urges and cooperate for the common good. In other words, they must reasonably conform to the code of behavior established, implemented, and administered by the organization and its managers, so that order is maintained and common goals can be accomplished.

In a formal organization, some pressures push toward conformity and uniformity, while counterpressures pull toward nonconformity and flexibility. The push-pull effect influences the formulation of policies and procedures as well as employee behavior. Conformity and uniformity result in short-term high efficiency, though individuality and creativity often suffer. Nonconformity results in short-term inefficiency, though individuality and creativity may be high in the long term.

Does this mean that organizations should operate on principles of non-conformity and flexibility? Not necessarily. Too much flexibility and non-conformity without policies, programs, and procedures for guiding employee behavior will lead to chaos, and the results of chaos are collapse and failure. All organizations must develop disciplinary policies and procedures to maintain order, congruity, and continuity. When disciplinary policies, procedures, and guidelines are vague or nonexistent, employees, not knowing the boundaries of acceptable behavior, will experience anxiety and apprehension. This leads to defensive or aggressive behavior. Likewise, when disciplinary policies are perceived as unfair, employees develop feelings of injustice about the way they are treated.

People have always been concerned about justice and fair treatment;

and feelings of injustice and a sense of grievance have been the underlying causes of most if not all revolutions. It can be said that two principles have maintained the American democratic process and free enterprise system: the opportunity to be upwardly mobile and share in the wealth of the nation; and the establishment of basic human rights, protected and maintained by legislation and due process. Managers at all levels must understand that when people believe they have been treated unfairly, they will, if their reasons are sufficiently strong, be motivated to seek redress, justice, or revenge.

Approaches to Discipline

Discipline provides a means to bring about a change in behavior based on authority or power. Disciplinary situations arise when a person has violated the norms of acceptable behavior of the organization. Norms may be implicit or explicit rules of behavior or methods of operation. Implicit norms are more subtle and often more difficult to understand than explicit norms. They can be inferred only from the behavior of others in the organization.

There are three basic meanings of the word *discipline:* (1) training that corrects, molds, strengthens, or perfects; (2) control gained by enforcing obedience; and (3) punishment or chastisement. If meanings (1) and (2) are combined, it can be stated that discipline involves the conditioning or molding of behavior by applying rewards and penalties. The third meaning is narrower because it pertains only to the act of punishing.

The first definition connotes a positive, constructive, or rehabilitative approach. This is discipline that managers at all levels should strive for. Positive discipline is actually broader and more fundamental than the definition implies; it involves the creation of attitudes and of an organizational climate that encourage employees to willingly conform to established rules and regulations. Its application, however, frequently requires considerable personal responsibility and self-discipline. It is achieved when management helps the employee change the undesired behavior and willingly accept and conform to the desired behavior. Positive discipline emphasizes internalization of the desire to do what is correct and in consonance with prevailing norms.

The second and third meanings of *discipline* include the use or threat of penalties to influence people to obey orders and live up to the rules of the system. Its application always requires social discipline. As we all know, psychological and social force are universally used.

Most employees who experience problems on the job, whether or not the cause is job-related, are able to change on their own and avoid having management initiate disciplinary action. However, if employee behavior must be corrected and effective solutions are sought, cause and motivation for the misbehavior should be identified. This, unfortunately, does not always seem possible or worth the effort; in such cases, solutions are often directed merely at symptoms. This is a hit-and-miss approach that can bring about unintended side effects.

Many supervisors avoid behavior problems because of pressure to maintain work output, concerns about lawsuits, intervention by government agencies and possible arbitration, fear of no support from higher levels of management, and even fear of physical harm.

In correcting employee misbehavior, either the positive or negative approach can be taken. Traditionally, the negative, or punitive, approach has been favored, and it is still the most widely used. The typical formal, progressive discipline in use today relies on warnings, threats, and suspensions. It is punishment oriented. In contrast, the positive approach is rehabilitative. It emphasizes personal responsibility and self-control. Under the punitive approach, employees learn to respond out of fear. Fear is a significant and effective influence on behavior; however, as fear diminishes, so does its effectiveness. Employees learn to avoid getting caught, or when caught they look for ways to retaliate.

Using a positive approach requires more patience and skill, but in the long term it often produces desired results—namely a more permanent positive change in an employee's behavior. This approach uses counseling, training, retraining, probation in lieu of suspension from work, reducing or removing barriers that inhibit performance, and emphasizing the need for individuals to take responsibility. Transferring, demoting, or ignoring the employee; denying privileges; withholding merit salary increases; and the use of peer pressure can be either punitive or rehabilitative, depending on how they are applied.

The degree of flexibility inherent in an organization's disciplinary program establishes the parameters supervisors have to operate within. The scope of authority is also influenced by the degree of independent authority supervisors have, as well as by tradition, customers, and present policies and practices.

Discipline programs that embody the merit principle usually have provision for using a wide variety of methods. Following is a list of the forms of discipline.

Negative-Punitive Forms of Discipline

- Suspension from work without pay for a specific number of consecutive workdays
- Suspension from work without pay for a specific number of staggered scheduled workdays
- Ridicule, sarcasm, criticism, intimidation, and threats, used separately or in combination
- Assignment to unpleasant, undesirable, or dirty jobs
- Frequently informing employees at the last possible moment that they have been scheduled to work overtime
- Scheduling work seven days a week for extended periods
- Compulsory overtime—for example, scheduling ten- to twelve-hour days when seven to eight is the norm
- Requiring a public explanation or apology
- Purposely delaying disciplinary action
- Spontaneous or summary termination
- Eliminating the job
- Promotion or lateral transfer to obscurity
- Assigning no work

Punitive-Rehabilitative Forms of Discipline

- Verbal and written warnings
- Permanent transfer to another job
- Permanent transfer to another shift
- Frequent checks on an employee's job performance
- Discrimination in raises and promotions
- Denial of privileges
- Silent treatment
- Changing work assignments
- Peer pressure
- Demotion

Positive-Rehabilitative-Constructive Forms of Discipline

- Counseling
- Probation
- Decision leave—one day suspension with pay

- Flextime
- Temporary reduction in scheduled work time
- Training or retraining programs
- Periodic reorientation
- Participation in recommending discipline
- Shock reduction on suspension
- Leave of absence with or without required assistance by professionals

Establishing Just Cause

In imposing disciplinary action, it is management who shoulders the primary responsibility of showing that just cause or a legitimate basis exists. The rationale for this is as follows:

- Our culture and social values require that the accused is presumed innocent until proven guilty.
- Management initiates the disciplinary action for reasons known to the employer. If the employee had to first prove innocence, he or she would have to show innocence for anything at any time.
- Requiring that supervisors show substantive reasons for discipline minimizes the misuse of authority. Supervisors who can impose discipline without having to account for it are more likely to abuse their authority than those who must give an accounting.
- Proving cause for discipline is the first step in moving toward constructive corrective action.
- Showing cause significantly reduces the likelihood that disciplined employees will become martyrs among their peers.
- Being able to demonstrate cause can be used to strengthen employee relations and facilitates fair treatment of employees.
- As a defensive act, proving cause can be used to support a position if the matter is referred to a third party.
- In unionized organizations, most agreements contain a provision requiring that just cause for discipline exist before any action is taken.

In unionized organizations, where formal due process procedures almost always exist, supervisors usually have had more experience in proving cause for discipline. Discipline cases are the ones most frequently heard by arbitrators, and over the years the published decisions of arbitrators have established a foundation of knowledge to guide supervisors in substantiating just cause. These considerations to show cause will increasingly be applied in nonunionized organizations. In fact, judges and government administrative officers will apply even stricter standards because many either have training in the law or are responsible for interpreting and enforcing the law. This will be especially true if they are unfamiliar with the "common law of the shop," which is simply the standard employer-employee environment and framework.

In addition, standards employed by arbitrators largely reflect prevailing social values and employee perceptions of fairness. I am not suggesting that managements in nonunion organizations adopt arbitration as part of due process or rigidly adhere to the general standards employed by arbitrators in discipline cases. Arbitrators themselves vary somewhat in how they apply these standards. I do suggest that, to be in consonance with prevailing values, the law, and employee expectations, supervisors use the standards to guide their thoughts and actions, primarily to ensure a high degree of fairness to all concerned. Another reason for doing so is to be on solid ground if the matter cannot be satisfactorily resolved through internal due process and is appealed to a third party, in which case a supervisor will be called on to defend an action. It should be remembered that in discipline situations, especially where termination is involved, courts and government agencies tend to be more sympathetic to employees than to employers.

Though the primary burden of proof properly rests with management, disciplined employees cannot idly maintain their innocence. Regardless of who is judging the matter, employees must present oral testimony as well as written and other evidence to support their position, whether it be complete innocence, partial guilt, or that imposed discipline is overly severe.

Considerations for Determining Just Cause

• Employee responsibilities or standards of conduct should be known and understood by all. Employees cannot be expected to observe required standards of conduct if they are unaware of them or do not understand them. Ignorance of a rule is occasionally a legitimate defense.

It must be pointed out, however, that ignorance as a defense can be used only in situations where management has failed to make the rule known and where, by virtue of common sense, employees could not be expected to have known such behavior was unacceptable.

• The employee responsibilities, as written, should be directly related to the nature of the organization's operations and business environment. Employees cannot be required to conform to rules that are neither relevant nor make sense. However, employees can be required to conform to limits on dress, hair styles, and activities if such requirements are legitimately defensible for legal, safety, or business considerations.

• In relatively minor instances of misconduct, where only a verbal reprimand is warranted, no formal written warning should be issued. However, a record of the verbal warning and resulting discussion should be made.

• Whenever a formal charge of misconduct is warranted, the specific charges must be clearly stated in writing. Whenever possible, the specific written rules or policies violated should be cited.

• Employees who fail to abide by the rules must be forewarned of the possible consequences for continued misconduct. They must clearly understand that a positive change in behavior is expected and that action will be taken if it is not forthcoming. Exceptions to the necessity of forewarning are for such misbehavior as immoral conduct, fighting, falsification of records, coming to work or working under the influence of drugs or intoxicants, major theft, and gross insubordination. In such cases, by virtue of common sense, employees should know that one violation could result in discharge.

The word *could* instead of *would*, or *may* instead of *will*, should be used. Words like *would* or *will* leave no room for flexibility and thus the ability to apply judgment. When flexibility is absent, choices do not exist. If a rule states that any employee who uses, possesses, or is under the influence of any intoxicant will be fired regardless of quality and length of service, management is bound to fire anyone who is caught breaking the rule. Any exceptions would cripple the rule's enforceability.

• Except for instances where immediate action is required, a fair and impartial investigation of the employee's alleged misconduct should be carried out in a timely manner. When immediate action is required, the best procedure is to suspend the employee pending the results of the investigation. Suspension during an investigation would be proper, for example, where an employee responsible for handling finances is accused of misappropriation or embezzlement. If the investigation shows that the employee is completely innocent of any wrongdoing, compensation for all losses incurred should be made.

A timely investigation is one conducted within three to five workdays from the date misconduct occurred. Most investigations can be completed within a week, although some will take longer. Facts, testimony, and other evidence should be obtained while they are fresh. In addition, it is unfair to an employee charged with misconduct to have to undergo the stress associated with delayed investigation.

• The documented results of any investigation must produce sufficient evidence or proof of guilt to support charges and impose discipline. The degree of proof required is proportional to the seriousness of the misconduct, the employee's overall record of service, and related factors. Misconduct that could result in termination and seriously impair the employee's chances for future employment should require proof of guilt beyond reasonable doubt. This is not to imply that the rigid standards of absolute proof required by courts for criminal law cases must be met.

• In order to effect discipline, management must consistently enforce the organization's expressed standards of conduct. This does not mean that, because certain employees may have eluded discipline for known misconduct or misconduct that management should have known occurred, an employee now charged with the same or similar misconduct cannot be disciplined. It means, instead, that management cannot legitimately apply and enforce rules on a selective or subjective basis.

Determining the Extent of Proof Required

Whatever misconduct an employee is accused of, evidence must substantiate the charges and the extent of any action taken. Although this may be intuitively obvious, too many supervisors still impose discipline in the mistaken belief that facts are not required to support actions. The question is: How much evidence or proof of wrongdoing is needed to support specific degrees of discipline? In the prosecution of criminal cases in the courts, standards of proof under criminal law are required; in addition, technical rules of evidence are strictly applied. Some believe the same standards should be applied to the disciplining of employees, especially when termination occurs. Though much can be learned from the standards of proof required and rules of evidence used in the courtroom, strict adherence to them is impractical and unsound. The relationship between supervisors and employees is not quite the same as the relationship between prosecutors and defendants. The employer-employee relationship is broader, extending to all employees and lasting over time.

Supervisors should be guided by the following principle: The more serious the misconduct, the higher the degree of proof required to impose extreme forms or degrees of discipline. Serious discipline, including termination, should require proof of guilt beyond reasonable doubt before any final action is taken. Where less serious discipline is involved, somewhat lesser degrees of proof should be established.

Conducting an Impartial Investigation

The objective of any investigation involving employee misconduct is to gather sufficient information relevant to the situation or incident in order to:

- Determine whether a basis of fact exists to formally accuse the employee.
- Serve, if an accusation has already been made, as the basis of fact for determining if the accusation was warranted and if warranted, as the basis for initiating some type of discipline.
- Serve, if some type of disciplinary action has been effected, such as a suspension from duties pending the outcome of an investigation, as the basis for either sustaining or rescinding the action.
- Determine if a basis of fact exists for imposing discipline over and above what already may have been given relative to the misconduct investigated.

In conducting an investigation, management should attempt to reconstruct as completely as possible the facts and circumstances that (1) preceded the situation or incident, (2) occurred during its course, and (3) took place after it occurred. Management should also attempt to learn about all mitigating facts and circumstances that have a bearing on the case. The investigation should provide answers to the following questions:

- *Who was involved?* The identities of all people directly and indirectly involved in the matter should be established. Whatever they know, say, or heard should be recorded for purposes of assessing the situation, identifying causes and effects, and determining possible courses of action.
- *What happened?* What caused the situation to become a disciplinary matter? Did it progress in stages over time or quickly arise?
- *What other factors were involved?* Does the matter pertain to or involve any one or a combination of the following—the employee's relationship with his or her peers and supervisors, the employee's responsi-

bilities, the employee's physical or emotional health, the employee's life outside the work place?
- *When and where did the incident occur?* Specific times, dates, and locations must be established.
- *Is there a pattern?* Is the employee's misconduct a singular act or part of a series? To what extent, if any, are the employee's associates or supervisors factors?
- *Why did the misconduct occur?* Was the employee's misbehavior intentional or unintentional? Did the employee act in good faith? Were his or her actions justified, partly justified, or totally unjustified? To what extent, if any, did management knowingly or unknowingly contribute to the employee's misconduct?
- *Is the employee sorry?* Is the employee repentant, and, if so, is it because of being caught or for other reasons?

The answers to these and other questions should be used not only to establish just cause but also to help management determine the appropriate type and degree of corrective action.

Information used for carrying out discipline should be documented and be able to withstand careful scrutiny. Written records should be made because they have an important advantage over verbal testimony. Time and circumstances tend to affect perceptions and memory, and written records reduce the likelihood of this occurring. Records compiled during or after an investigation should be witnessed and signed if they will be directly or indirectly used to provide a basis for disciplinary action. Written records should also be systematically developed in sufficient detail so as to clearly communicate the intended information and meaning.

The Disciplinary Interview

The disciplinary interview is a central element in the discipline process. Without it, guilt or innocence is determined without the benefit of hearing the employee's position and weighing its merits. If the employee is judged guilty, discipline is imposed without proper evaluation of factors and/or conditions in his or her favor. If no internal procedure exists for seeking redress, the employee is denied the right to due process within the organization. The employee must then choose between accepting management's decision or taking the matter outside the organization and pursuing due process in another forum.

For all concerned, it is best to allow the employee to have his or her "day in court" before passing judgment on the matter and taking corrective action. Furthermore, giving the employee the opportunity to respond to charges before judgment is passed, determining what action (if any) is appropriate, and deciding what needs to be done to prevent a recurrence cannot be properly accomplished without discussion with the employee.

If properly planned and carried out, the interview or meeting can:

- Foster the notion of personal responsibility and self-discipline.
- Facilitate improved communication by clearing the air of possible misunderstandings.
- Ensure that the employee's rights are safeguarded.
- Serve to more accurately determine the employee's innocence or degree of guilt.
- Promote good employee relations.
- Provide a forum for the employee to explain the reasons for whatever caused the disciplinary matter.
- Serve as a basis for determining the appropriate corrective action.

Every disciplinary interview should be thoroughly planned. Supervisors should prepare facts, documents, and records and be aware of attitudes. As supervisor you may feel frustrated, angry, sympathetic, vindictive, or something else. The employee may feel guilty, indignant, persecuted, hurt, helpless, anxious, flip, cavalier, or belligerent. To increase the chances that an interview will be a positive experience, observe the following guidelines:

1. Organize and review all relevant and pertinent information obtained from the investigation, including documents, records, and testimony.
2. Set a time and place for the meeting. The meeting should be private, face-to-face, and attended by as few people as possible—preferably one-on-one.
3. In most cases, give the employee at least a day's advance notice about the meeting's time, place, and purpose.
4. Keep in mind that conducting the meeting in your office puts the employee at a psychological disadvantage. Unless a psychological advantage is desired, consider holding the meeting in a more neutral place, such as a conference room.
5. Consider the effect the arrangement of chairs, desks, spacial dis-

tance, and even ventilation and lighting could have on attitude and behavior.

6. Learn as much as is relevant and realistically possible about the employee's background, record of service, character, and attitude. This information should be used to plan the physical and psychological climate for the meeting.

7. Remember that judgment of guilt or innocence should not be made until the employee has been heard and listened to. Though it may be impossible not to have some feeling about the employee's guilt or innocence prior to the interview, prejudgment is a miscarriage of justice.

8. Control your own emotions and actions when conducting the interview.

9. If the employee is known to be hostile, intimidating, or a hothead, take steps prior to the meeting to induce the employee to exercise self-restraint or change. Let the employee know that if such behavior is shown it will hurt his or her case.

Remember the purpose of the meeting, despite your frustration or anger:

- To outline the problem and whatever charges have been made
- To present the known facts pertaining to the matter
- To give the employee an opportunity to explain his or her position and views
- If possible at the time, to decide on the employee's degree of guilt or innocence; if the matter needs to be given further thought or a reinvestigation is called for, judgment should not be passed during the meeting
- To decide corrective action if the employee is judged culpable
- To work out an approach to constructively resolve the matter and avoid recurrence

It is more common for an employee accused of misconduct, be it for breaking a rule, absenteeism, poor performance, or anything else, to feel anxious. This is not bad, especially if the employee knows that he or she is guilty—guilt can serve as an effective incentive to change behavior. So can fear. However, behavioral changes arising out of fear work only if the fear is maintained. If an employee is extremely anxious, nervous, or depressed, he or she needs to know that the world is not coming to an end. Even if termination is possible, the employee's dignity and sense of self-worth do not have to be destroyed in the process. Employees need to understand the purposes of a disciplinary interview and be convinced of management's belief in rehabilitative discipline.

Guidelines for the Interview's Setting

The following are offered to guide supervisors in creating the type of mood and setting that will best serve their purposes. There is no one best way for each employee or form of misconduct. Many factors will affect the setting and climate of the interview, such as the sense of urgency and the supervisor's preferred style. The arrangement of information on the supervisor's desk can affect the psychological climate. The supervisor whose desk is orderly, with necessary records closely at hand, projects the image of a person who is organized, prepared, and in control. To the employee, this can be assuring or intimidating.

The supervisor, whether male or female, who wears a suit jacket and addresses the employee as Mr., Mrs., or Ms., instead of by first name, establishes a formal atmosphere. The supervisor whose jacket is off and shirt sleeves are rolled up, and who goes on a first name basis, creates an informal setting.

The soft light of a desk lamp creates a different mood from that of harsh overhead fluorescent lights. Drawing office blinds or drapes can make the employee feel comfortable or uncomfortable. How close the supervisor sits to the employee while conversing can affect the meeting. The closer the supervisor is to the employee, the more likely the employee will feel anxious.

Beginning the Interview

If the employee's situation is not serious, the meeting should usually be informal, low-key, and friendly. Don't stay behind the desk; instead, sit three to five feet from the employee. Avoid strong words and emotions. The tone of conversation should be nonthreatening—one of discovery and examination. Taking written notes during the meeting is optional; making mental notes is essential.

When the employee's situation is serious, be direct and formal. Stay behind the desk and even stand while the employee is seated. The agenda should have been thoroughly planned, and a wider range of feelings should be displayed. Don't understate the seriousness of the matter; the employee should understand the consequences for failure to change. Note-taking is suggested as long as it does not interfere with listening. No matter how serious the matter, common courtesy should be extended and maintained.

Always start a disciplinary interview with a positive attitude. Opening remarks may be of a general nature, those typically used in starting a conversation, but keep remarks not related to the purpose of the meeting to a minimum. Their only purpose is to allow the employee to become acclimated to the setting and, if possible, to be somewhat at ease. Once the employee is settled, state the purpose of the meeting. In general, tell the employee:

- Why the meeting has been called. Do not assume that the employee fully understands why. Even if the reason is known, restating it will ensure that everyone is addressing the same issue.
- What specifically the individual has been charged with, accused of, or suspected of. If it's a job-performance problem, identify the specific deficiencies believed to exist. If it's an attendance problem, state the specific amount of absence or lateness. If it's a violation of employee responsibilities or standards of conduct, state the specific improprieties.
- That a decision will not be made until after relevant facts have been examined and views expressed. If information is brought to light that changes the substance of the case, a decision about the employee's innocence or guilt may not be possible or feasible at the end of the meeting.
- If it is decided that misconduct has occurred, the objective of any corrective action is to avoid a repetition of the situation, incident, problem, or issue.

In evaluating the nonverbal communication that goes on, pay attention to the following:

• *Facial expressions*. During the course of an exchange, facial expressions will change as the employee reacts to what is said. The smile, frown, pursed lips, scowl, raised eyebrow, thrusting chin, angle of the head in relation to the body, yawn, lip biting, and sneer all convey information.

• *Body posture*. During the course of a conversation, posture and body movement will change. Slouching may indicate disinterest while erectness could mean anxiety. Folded arms could show defensiveness. Cross legs, clasped hands, and fingers playing with a piece of jewelry all convey information.

• *Gestures.* Most people have certain hand movements they regularly use when talking. Some may be idiosyncratic while others have universal meaning.

• *Eye contact.* Eye contact is an important facet of communication. Eye contact and expressions show in the eyes, coupled with facial expressions and other nonverbal communication, are strong signs of feeling. Avoidance of eye contact can signal shame, guilt, anxiety, insecurity, resentment, or fear. Eye contact can also signal when to talk, when the other person is about to speak, or when to keep quiet. Intense, prolonged eye contact (approximately ten seconds or longer) can show very strong positive or negative feelings.

A well-developed ability to read nonverbal communication will help you anticipate what the employee is going to say and how he or she is likely to act on what has been said.

Keep emotions under control. Letting emotions overtake logic, reason, and judgment is a major reason why disciplinary interviews fail to serve their intended purpose. Of course, maintaining control over emotions does not mean being devoid of emotion. Be sensitive to overreacting or overexpressing yourself. Be honest and sincere yet tactful—if you are not, it will show in your speech and body language. The employee will be quick to sense it and will react in a self-protective way.

Presenting the Evidence

Once you determine the employee understands the nature and purpose of the interview, present the facts at hand. It is most important to stick to the issue and facts; avoid rambling or talking about unrelated issues. If the situation involves patterned or cumulative misconduct, make reference to the continuing problem. Use caution, however, because the employee may be innocent or only partly to blame. Proceed to tell the employee what facts, records, documents, testimony, and so on have been obtained to indicate cause for discipline. Remember that the employee may not accept the fact that a problem exists. The employee may view his or her behavior as normal or something that management is making an unnecessarily big deal about.

It is important that you take the time to help the employee understand that a problem or potential problem is believed to exist. If the employee admits, or prior to the meeting has admitted, misconduct it is not necessary to present all the information that has been obtained. There is no need for overkill. Present enough information to show that relative to the seriousness of the matter, sufficient reason exists for taking corrective action.

After the evidence of specific misconduct has been presented, or if charges have already been substantiated, give the employee the opportunity to respond. If the employee admits to wrongdoing, the case is made and the next step is to find out why it happened. If the employee proclaims innocence of any and all wrongdoing, he or she now bears the burden of proof. If partial responsibility or culpability is admitted, the employee must explain why. Again, the employee now has the responsibility to present a defense.

Listen carefully with an open mind to what the employee has to say. If necessary, take notes. It is not unusual for the employee's and supervisor's interpretations of the "facts" to differ. Avoid getting into an argument or debate. The employee may say that information was overlooked, relevant factors and conditions were ignored or not properly considered, the record is wrong, or others have not told the truth. The employee's defense can include just about anything and everything. This is where the value of knowing the employee and having done a thorough investigation are most important.

If the employee's understanding of the matter differs from your own, clarify the areas where agreement exists and where there is disagreement. Again, avoid getting defensive and emotional; neither will be productive. Stick to the issue and the facts. It's easy to go off on tangents, talk about vague and nonrelated issues, and even get into an argument.

Most employees will be sincere and honest. They will honestly believe that they are right in their opinions and beliefs. It is essential to have well-developed interpersonal skills to work through this part of the interview without damaging the relationship. Remember, only a small percentage of employees are real troublemakers, argumentative, dishonest, deceptive, aggressive, or otherwise cause problems. Here the discussion concerns a basically good employee, who with counseling and constructive discipline is likely to self-correct. Remember, the purpose of the discipline is rehabilitative. Only a small percentage of employees are destined for termination.

If what the employee has said causes you to doubt the accuracy or credibility of your position, tell the employee you need to do some further investigation. Close the meeting and let the employee know you will be in touch within a specified time period.

If you are convinced that the employee's position lacks merit, tactfully but firmly say so. Help the employee see that his or her position is contrary to what you believe are the facts. If it appears the employee is not listening, or that an argument is in the making, back off and bring the discussion to a close. Assuming that an internal due process system exists, the employee has the right to appeal your action if he or she is dissatisfied with the outcome of the meeting and subsequent action.

An employee's guilt or innocence and the degree thereof should be decided after a disciplinary interview has been conducted. In some cases, after the employee has expressed his or her position, a determination can be made during the interview. In others, reinvestigation is indicated and a second interview will be necessary. And in still others, you will want to reflect on the interview and weight many factors in deciding on the type and degree of discipline that should be given.

Deciding on Specific Discipline

All employees must be judged by the same standards, and rules must apply equally to all working under the same policies and in similar work environments. This does not mean that the same disciplinary action must be taken with all employees who are guilty of the same or similar misconduct, however. Disciplinary action should be consistent, but it must be given according to the individual situation. This is one of the most difficult ideas for supervisors to properly apply in practice. To achieve consistency in a program that provides for merit, the following factors should be considered.

The Seriousness of the Misconduct

Misconduct falls into two categories: major offenses, for which an employee can be fired; and minor offenses, usually requiring something less than termination. The minimum and maximum discipline that can be imposed for each type of misconduct should be spelled out as part in any discipline program. By establishing minimums and maximums, necessary parameters are established that help achieve a high level of consistency. For some types of misconduct the parameters may be broad, while for others they may be narrow.

An example of a major offense would be use, possession, or being under the influence of an intoxicant. For such misconduct the range of discipline is likely to be narrow. It would be illogical to give a verbal warning as minimum discipline. Instead, the minimum might be a lengthy suspension or probation, while the maximum would be termination. In this example, flexibility is limited.

An example of a minor offense would be failing to follow the proper procedure for requisitioning material from stock. The minimum discipline would likely be a verbal reprimand, while the maximum might be a written warning and possibly some time off without pay. This wider range of choice for discipline provides for more flexibility. Unless the employee was a repeat offender or had a cumulative record of misconduct, discharging someone for such misconduct would be far too severe.

The discharge of an employee who continually violates the minor rules is handled by a policy statement to the effect that "frequent, cumulative, or excessive violation of any one or a combination of the rules will be cause for possible termination." An employee approaching this point must be clearly forewarned that he or she is close to being fired.

If no parameters exist, or if they range from a verbal warning to termination for each written employee responsibility, individual managers' evaluations of specific situations will likely vary so widely that they will be indefensibly inconsistent. Parameters and written criteria with guidelines for their evaluation will help to ensure consistency while retaining flexibility for applying merit.

The Employee's Record of Conduct

An employee with a record of little or no misconduct, other things being equal, is likely to receive minimum discipline for a first offense. If there is a record of misconduct, the length of time since the last occurrence must be considered. As a rule of thumb, prior minor misconduct should not be considered if more than twelve months have passed since it last occurred. Serious misconduct should be considered if it occurred within the past eighteen to twenty-four months. Time periods should be based not on a calendar year, where on December 31 all discipline during the past year is erased, but on an anniversary year. Organizations that use the calendar year often must clear the record of employees who on December 31 are on the verge of discharge. Frequently, these employees continue misbehaving and again come close to discharge by December 31, but on January 1 again start with clean records.

For supervisors who are caught in this dilemma, the following suggestion is offered. Though most policy statements and negotiated labor agreements state that specific reference to instances of previous misconduct cannot be used if they are more than a year old, management can refer to general patterned misbehavior without citing specifics. For example, suppose employee Tisone has continually gotten herself to the edge of being fired by December 31. The labor agreement says that all records must be wiped clean on January 1. As usual, Tisone starts misbehaving in January. This time her discipline should not be minimal; it should be closer to the maximum. Without referencing any specific previous misbehavior, she should be told verbally and in writing that because of her well-established pattern of misconduct and failure to respond positively to continuing effects to rehabilitate her, severe action is warranted.

What about recurrences of misconduct within a single year? Time between occurrences of misbehavior must be considered in prescribing discipline. Some organizations use stated fixed periods in deciding whether to increase the level of discipline. For example, a repeat of misconduct within ninety days of the first occurrence would warrant the next step in discipline. With this approach, however, the employee who repeats within eighty-nine days gets the next level of discipline, while the one who repeats in ninety-one days receives the same discipline as given for the first occurrence. Generally, the longer an employee goes without getting into trouble, the more it should be counted in his or her favor. Therefore, approximate time periods are recommended. This gives supervisors flexibility and effectively deals with the employee who waits until the proverbial ninety-first day before repeating misconduct.

The Employee's Length and Quality of Service

A long-term employee with a good service record would certainly receive lesser discipline for the same misconduct than a short-term employee with a poor service record. Most organizations have fixed probation periods during which a new employee can be dismissed if he or she fails in any way to perform or behave as required. In unionized organizations, bargaining-unit employees are usually denied seniority rights—that is, union protection— until after probation is successfully completed. Once it is completed the employee starts accruing job rights—he or she begins accumulating deposits in an organizational bank account. The same applies to employees in non-union organizations. Once probation is successfully completed, an implied contract for continued employment exists between the employer and the employee.

Most personnel policy manuals and employee handbooks contain language to the effect that once probation is completed, the employee enjoys permanent status, participates in benefits, accrues certain rights based on seniority, and most important, can only be dismissed for cause. Supervisors have to live by these written words. The longer this implied contractual relationship exists, the stronger it becomes. Management must take this into account when determining discipline.

For all intents and purposes, a short-term employee's investment in the organization and the organization's investment in the individual is minimal. Management is not obligated to spend considerable time, energy, and money attempting to rehabilitate a short-term employee.

The Employee's Position in the Organization

Generally, higher-level employees should be held to a higher standard of conduct because these employees are highly visible and their behavior impacts heavily on the organization. This is particularly true with respect to managers.

If people in highly responsible jobs, especially those with authority and leadership, do not set and maintain the standards for proper conduct, who will? When standard-bearers who misbehave are not disciplined, respect for management and authority will erode. Because of their roles and responsibilities, employees in higher-level positions can be subject to more severe discipline than those in less visible and responsible jobs who are guilty of the same misconduct.

Changes in Behavior as a Result of Previous Discipline

Changes in behavior must be evaluated in light of the seriousness of the problem and what has been done to deal with it. A long-standing problem is usually more difficult to correct than one of recent origin. If no progress has been made, the approach should be changed. If progress is impossible— say, because of physical or mental impairment—management should consider transfer to a more suitable position. Disability retirement or medical separation may also have to be considered. If some progress has occurred but the employee has relapsed to old ways, the time span and degree of change will have to be weighed against what effort has been spent and what has been gained. A major relapse in a short period after extensive rehabilitation could justify serious consideration of demotion or separation.

The Employee's Physical and Mental Health

An employee's problem may be caused by physical or mental impairment. If the problem is temporary, a probable recovery rate can be projected by qualified medical personnel. If recovery is impossible or only partly achievable, and the employee cannot meet the standards required of others in similar jobs, removal will have to be considered. In a competitive world it is unrealistic to guarantee employees lifetime employment regardless of their inability to meet reasonable performance standards. Others capable of performing the work must eventually assume the duties of the incapacitated employee. Partial and sometimes full lifetime income is guaranteed by the array of disability insurance provided by the employer, private insurance, and the government.

Motives for Misconduct

An employee's motive is an important consideration. Though ignorance cannot totally excuse misconduct, whether the employee knew right from wrong should be considered. Ignorance based on inadequate or faulty training should not be counted against the employee. Nor should situations beyond the employee's control. But where the employee clearly understood or reasonably should have understood right from wrong, such can be counted against the employee. The same applies when misconduct is intentional. Willful neglect is most serious, whereas justifiable ignorance can be viewed as least serious—incompetence falls somewhere between the two. Incompetence because of faulty training is one thing, but incompetence because of faulty learning is quite another.

In considering motives for misconduct, supervisors must carefully document the particulars and have sound reasons to support the weighting given to such factors.

Past and Present Disciplinary Policies and Practices

Circumstances can result in management's changing disciplinary policies and practices. Leniency in discipline, even condoning such misconduct as absence and lateness, can be reversed and vice versa. The reasons for changing policies and practices should be communicated to employees so they will have sufficient time to adapt. Generally, sudden crackdowns are unfair and expectations of instant change are unrealistic. It is important that whatever action is taken conform to current policies and practices. If management is tightening up heretofore loose practices, what was formerly seen as minor and given minimal discipline will now be viewed as more serious and warranting moderate discipline. If management has been lax in enforcing a rule, inconsistency can render the rule unenforceable. To remedy this, management could inform all employees that beginning on a certain date the rule will be vigorously enforced, or deactivate the existing rule and replace it with a revised rule that actually means the same as the old rule.

Similar Cases

Guidelines are necessary to show how consistency in handling similar cases could be achieved under a merit program. Written guidelines, training, follow-up monitoring, record keeping, and discrimination of information about how specific cases were handled are all necessary.

Mitigating or Aggravating Circumstances

It would be an injustice not to consider how mitigating or aggravating circumstances may have directly caused or contributed to the disciplinary situation. The degree to which such circumstances can influence the determination of discipline must be weighed in proportion to all other relevant factors. When such circumstances are considered, documentation must be part of the record. Consideration of extenuating factors, however, cannot be allowed to become a permanent psychological crutch for an employee. At some point the chronically troubled employee must overcome or control whatever difficulties are contributing to behavior and/or performance problems.

The Employee's Replaceability

An organization should not permit any employee, however valuable, to become irreplaceable. Sometimes, however, it does occur. It would be an injustice to all other employees to allow any individual to "act beyond the law" because of his or her value to the organization. In the short term, management may feel compelled to give an irreplaceable employee less discipline than others for the same misconduct. This is a very dangerous course of action. If an "irreplaceable" employee continues to misbehave, a suitable replacement should be sought. If one cannot be found, then management must show the good sense and courage to treat the employee no differently than anyone else, even though the employee may either leave or retaliate.

The Employee's Popularity

In most organizations problem employees are usually the least popular, but this is not always the case. Severely disciplining a very popular employee can bring about a negative reaction from other employees. In theory, popularity, like irreplaceability, should not be considered. However, *not* considering popularity can be very expensive. In the short term, management may feel compelled to give a popular employee more latitude and be more lenient in imposing discipline. However, to do so sends the wrong message to other employees and erodes the respect good employees have for management. A popular troublesome employee should be quickly identified and ways to change perceptions implemented. On the other hand, a popular employee may risk losing status if others perceive him or her as a discipline problem. Advising the employee of this should not be overlooked, nor should the use of peer pressure be ignored.

Can the Case Against the Employee Survive Review?

Possible review should be the last factor considered. If everything is done correctly, the case should survive reviews. All too often, however, supervisors ask this question first. This is wrong. Government administrators, judges, and arbitrators do not manage organizations; managers do. But managers must manage in ways that are in consonance with the law and with prevailing social values. It is recognized that outsiders will occasionally yield to political pressure, make honest mistakes, and modify or even rescind proper discipline. When this occurs, management should seriously consider exercising appeal rights.

Based on all the aforementioned, the specific type and degree of discipline should be decided. Once the decision is made, it should be communicated verbally and in writing to the employee. Though others may have participated in assessing the situation, the employee's immediate supervisor should play a major role in the process.

Communicating the Decision

Once the decision is made, schedule a meeting with the employee. Tell the employee of the decision and the basis for it. If the employee becomes argumentative, advise the individual of rights of appeal and end the meeting. If, as in most cases, the employee accepts the news in a mature manner, discussion should ensue to ascertain how recurrences can be avoided. The employee must clearly understand what the organization will or will not do to minimize the likelihood of a repetition. The employee must also understand the degree to which his or her status has been affected in the short and long term.

An attempt should be made to show the employee that the discipline being imposed is in both the organization's and his or her best interests. Though the employee may not always see it this way, management should endeavor to work toward that end.

Express confidence in the employee's ability to exercise personal responsibility and, to the extent necessary, take the appropriate steps to change behavior. Advise the employee that if the problem persists or others requiring discipline arise, further action will result and present misconduct will be considered as part of the total record. Make summary notes of the meeting and keep them on file. As necessary, schedule a follow-up meeting.

Present a formal letter of discipline to the employee. It can be given during the meeting, at the end, or shortly thereafter. It is essential that the letter contain the following:

- The basis for cause to discipline
- Specific violations of rules or employee responsibilities or acts of misconduct
- The extent to which previous misconduct is being considered in the present situation
- The results of the investigation of the matter
- The specific form and degree of corrective action being imposed or taken
- Expectations for changes in behavior
- The period for which discipline will be retained as part of the employee's permanent record
- Forewarning that if the need for discipline persists, it will be viewed in a more serious manner and require further corrective action
- The employee's right to appeal if dissatisfied with the action

The primary purpose of all disciplinary action is to get employees to make permanent, positive changes in their behavior. Most employees are responsible people who, on rare occasion, violate some expressed or implied standard of conduct. For these employees, personal responsibility and self-discipline should be stressed. Irresponsible employees usually have to be punished and controlled. Before any disciplinary action can be taken, just cause must first be established. Once just cause is established, any discipline should be given according to what is merited.

9

Employee Performance Appraisal

It is an inherent responsibility of those in managerial positions to pass judgment on what employees do with respect to meeting job requirements. While individual employees are responsible for their own performance, it is supervisors who shoulder overall responsibility for the performance of the unit under their direction. As I have said throughout this book, employees work for self-serving reasons, and employers hire and retain employees for self-serving reasons. The employer's and employee's commitment to each other is based on the axiom: "What has each done for the other lately?" In order to determine who has contributed what, some mechanisms need to exist. *Compensation management* is the most appropriate term to identify the field of activities and its various mechanisms. The three major activities are: job evaluation, salary structuring, and performance appraisal. In this book, I discuss the last of these.

The Purpose and Nature of Performance Appraisal

The activity that is most difficult to administer is performance appraisal. In fact, appraising or judging employee performance is one of the most difficult aspects of managing. Most organizations profess to use merit—job performance—as the primary criterion for rewarding employees. In reality, most merit systems do not work out that way. It seems self-evident that because money is such an important influencer of job-related behavior, employees adjust their behavior to acquire salary increases. Those in management who believe that salary increases should not be related to job performance fail to understand, or do not want to accept, the importance of money to most employees. Employees should clearly understand that all forms of rewards—whether money, promotions, privileges, or status symbols—are directly related to their performance. If in practice rewards are given on bases other than job performance, an employee's time and energy will likely be directed accordingly in order to gain the desired rewards, and performance will suffer.

Because most performance-appraisal programs do not work as they should, supervisors often become frustrated to the point where they give the same percentage salary increases to virtually all employees. This all-too-common practice encourages mediocrity. It takes a tremendous amount of time and energy to design, implement, and manage an effective performance-appraisal program. But if it is done correctly, the benefits of reduced costs and increased productivity greatly exceed development and maintenance costs.

One major reason for the failure of more performance-appraisal programs is that the systems are poorly designed. Some of the flaws in design are (1) use of wrong performance criteria; (2) vague definitions of performance criteria; (3) vague definitions of degrees of performance; and (4) failure to weigh performance factors.

While most systems can stand to be improved, even a well-designed system can fail to function properly simply because people are what they are. Some of the human and environmental variables that frequently contribute to problems are:

- Prejudices and biases of assessors
- Political gaming skills of employees
- Attitudes of management and employees toward performance appraisal
- Political pressures to statistically skew appraisals to the high or low side, or even to maintain a normal distribution
- Lack of training in how to judge performance
- Lack of absolute or relative measures of employee performance
- Absence of controls to curb approval of biased appraisals
- Ineffectiveness of existing controls
- Lack of correlation among the results of performance appraisals, raises, promotions, and other forms of rewards
- Lack of discipline for employees whose performance is below standard

Any performance-appraisal program in which all levels of management do not fully support rewards based on performance is destined to fall short of what is desirable. The philosophy of the people at the top of any organization should set the basic tone and pattern for the organization's operational behavior.

Performance appraisal usually means the formal process or act of measuring how well an employee has handled assigned duties and responsibilities during a given period of time. Performance appraisals are used for a variety of purposes, including compensation administration, promotional consideration, disciplinary consideration, transfer, layoff, career-pathing, and assessing training needs. One of the most important benefits to be gained from performance appraisal is the strengthening of relationships between supervisors and employees.

The person who has the primary responsibility for judging employee performance is the supervisor. Most supervisors have little, if any, training in how to properly assess employee performance, and this causes no end of problems. Performance appraisal is not a once-a-year process, where a supervisor dusts off some form created by the human resources department and goes through the process of checking boxes and writing a few comments. It is a continuous part of the day-to-day working relationship between a supervisor and employees.

Most supervisors do not get highly enthused about having to formally assess employee performance. In fact, many would rather not do it at all. They give all types of reasons: "It is not important"; "I know my people"; "I do not have the time." These excuses and many other defense mechanisms show that some supervisors are at best apprehensive and at worst terrified of having a face-to-face discussion with employees about their performance. They are, essentially, afraid of getting into a situation where they cannot cope with the possible consequences.

Most employees want feedback on how they are performing in relation to standards or expectations. They also expect to be rewarded for their contributions to the organization. An organization must develop a performance-appraisal system that can consistently and, if properly used, relatively accurately measure employee performance. It goes without saying that rewards must be geared to performance. It is the responsibility of higher management to thoroughly train supervisors in conducting appraisals, and to ensure that the learning is correctly applied. Supervisors must understand that their own performance appraisals are in part based on how well they can assess the performance of employees.

The keys to doing successful performance appraisals are: (1) that employees understand what is expected of them; (2) that they are informally assessed on an ongoing basis; (3) that they are appropriately rewarded or disciplined; and (4) that they have a right to discuss their feelings and concerns.

Judging employee performance is often referred to as "letting them know where they stand." But information on where employees stand is subject to interpretation. It is similar to asking a person how he or she feels. It's a relative thing. Letting an employee know where he or she stands normally refers to the employee's position in relation to other employees, or the employee's position in relation to standards which he or she is being compared to.

Not all employees favor formal appraisals. Poor or marginal employees especially dislike them. Employees whose job performance is viewed via subjective standards recognize that judgments based on impressions or gut feelings can vary widely. Lastly, employees who receive built-in feedback automatically on their performance tend to see little useful purpose in a formal review.

Before any performance-appraisal program can be developed and implemented, employees must understand the responsibilities and duties of their job, the purpose of performance appraisals, the bases on which their performance is judged, and the rewards and discipline given in conjunction with performance or lack thereof. They must also know their rights of appeal for perceived unfairness and the channels and procedures to be followed in an appeal.

Any employee's formal performance appraisal is influenced, even sometimes predetermined, by events and conditions that occur long before the face-to-face meeting. Relationships between supervisors and employees are important. If a supervisor and an employee cannot express their feelings and opinions without reasonable candor, then the performance-appraisal meeting will be approached with reluctance, suspicion, even fear. The fewer surprises that occur for supervisors and employees in an appraisal meeting, the more effective the appraisal will be for all. It is primarily the supervisor's responsibility to establish and maintain a climate where accurate, timely, and open communication can exist.

Supervisors and employees who have poor working relationships will find the appraisal experience painful. In this climate, more problems are created or inflated than are discussed and resolved. Under these considerations, it may be better not to have the supervisor conduct the appraisal. This does not mean that the employee relationship problem will go away; eventually it will worsen. In this type of environment, time and money could be better spent correcting basic relationship problems than in concentrating on appraisals. Once the climate improves, an appraisal program can be implemented to strengthen the relationship.

Performance appraisal is composed of two parts—observation and evaluation—and both are subject to potential bias. Whatever type of system or approach is used, the possibility exists that bias and prejudice will affect judgments. Bias and prejudice may be caused by poor system design, interpersonal conflict, differing expectations, and various situational and organizational factors.

Overcoming Common Performance-Appraisal Problems

A valid and reliable system, with comprehensive training for all levels of management in the conducting of performance appraisals, is essential. Factors affecting performance appraisals must be recognized and barriers either overcome or controlled.

Lack of knowledge about what an employee is responsible for, or what an employee has or has not accomplished during a given period of time, is a common problem. This is why position descriptions and performance standards are essential. However, unless supervisors interact frequently with employees to monitor performance, problems will occur. This doesn't mean that a supervisor must go to every employee daily and find out how many beans they have counted that day. Trying to be that precise is more akin to harassment than to managing. However, some types of jobs do require daily monitoring, or bean counting.

Good employees require less monitoring than poor employees. Yet good employees should not be ignored because they are doing their jobs well. Their behavior and performance needs to be reinforced occasionally by letting them know they are doing well. Poor employees need to understand they must change their behavior or suffer the consequences for poor performance.

Supervisors, like all other people, have their biases and prejudices. Learn to control your personal feelings and remain objective. Prime examples of prejudice in performance appraisals are age, job tenure or seniority, gender, religion, ethnic origin, and race. Like everyone else, you have a tendency to characterize and stereotype people. Such stereotyping as these are common:

- Men are better suited or qualified to do this type of work. Therefore, it is obvious that a man will do a better job than a woman. Examples

might include operating heavy equipment, driving a forging hammer, cupola loading in a foundry, or stevedoring on a dock.
- Women are better suited or qualified to do this type of work. Therefore, it is obvious that a woman will do a better job than a man. Examples might include secretary, file clerk, switchboard operator, receptionist, airplane flight attendant.
- Older employees have reached their full potential. Therefore, we should not waste time training and developing them for higher levels of work. Besides, they will be leaving us soon.
- Young employees have more potential to develop than older employees. They should receive the training and development.
- Young employees are immature. We can't give them high levels of authority and responsibility until they are older. They must have a few gray hairs to show they have matured.

Besides the possible violations of law, there are practical reasons such biases should not be demonstrated. When employees recognize that obtaining rewards is based on things over which they have no control, problems surface. The best way to minimize these biases is to demonstrate that they are not considerations in judging performance.

Performance appraisals are also affected by situational and organizational factors. For instance, an employee's popularity can affect his or her appraisal. It is easier to judge an unpopular employee as a poor performer than to judge a popular the same way. An employee's relationship with others, especially higher-level managers, is a significant factor.

Employees' or supervisors' perceptions of how rewards are really given rather than how they are theoretically given is another factor. Employees at any level will rationalize all types of behavior to obtain rewards. If apple polishing or boot licking is the name of the game, then this will be the behavior many will exhibit. Those who refuse to play the game, or do not know how, can become jealous or resentful. The most effective way to deal with this is to make certain that performance is the name of the game, and it is the only game in the organization.

How closely employees work with their supervisors can influence a performance appraisal. The saying "out of sight, out of mind" is appropriate. Employees who work closely with their supervisors are able to influence the supervisor's perceptions almost continually. If they create a bad impression one day, they can change it in short order. Employees who do not see their supervisors often have no such advantage. The supervisor's impressions are formed by what others say, or when interaction does occur. Of course, the opposite could also exist. Employees who project a positive image and who do not see their supervisors often have less of a chance of a supervisor's perceptions changing than employees who are seen by their supervisor daily.

The availability of rewards is another factor affecting appraisals. When rewards are scarce, there is a tendency to spread them evenly across the board. The rationale is that since there is so little to go around, it does not pay to differentiate among employees. The same logic can also apply when rewards are plentiful. Having done well, management can afford to be generous. In times of high inflation and limited money for raises, the desire for raises across the board can be very strong. The best way to handle this problem is to give raises and other rewards solely on the basis of merit, or to give a small percentage across the board and the remainder on merit. As an example, if a supervisor is allotted 5 percent of his budget for raises, he could give 5 percent across the board. This, of course, would create mediocrity. It would be better to discriminate among employees on the basis of merit. A high performer might receive 10 percent and a low performer might receive nothing.

Employees learn to play upon their supervisor's sympathies to get larger raises and other rewards. For example, employees may avoid dressing in expensive clothing, complain about the high cost of living, drive an old car to work and remark on how it needs to be continually repaired because a new one is just too expensive, or pass remarks about how they cannot afford to pay for the children's education. These tactics tend to increase when performance-appraisal time draws near. The best way to handle this form of politicking is to ignore it. The more you react positively to these games, the more they will be played. Eventually it will lead to one-upmanship among employees. Employees will try to outdo their peers, and simultaneously try to discredit their peers' remarks.

Another class of barriers is tradition and past practice. Traditions like rewards for length of employment in the organization are not uncommon. A typical statement often heard is, "We take care of our senior employees." An employee's tenure of employment or seniority should not be heavily weighted for reward purposes. Traditions and past practices should be retained only if they facilitate or reinforce performance of employees.

Supervisors often permit their own values and perceptions to affect judgments about employee performance. For instance, supervisors may have thoughts like these:

- If I assess employee performance as below average, I am saying that I am an ineffective supervisor.

- I am an effective supervisor, therefore my employees do their jobs well.
- I have only high-performing employees on our team. I discharged the poor performers a long time ago.
- If I tell an employee that she is not doing well, it will have a negative effect on our relationship.
- If I get high raises for my employees, it will increase my effectiveness with them. They will perceive me as a supervisor who can get rewards for them.
- New employees in the unit should not be assessed as higher than average for the first couple of years. As time passes, I can assess them higher to show how they have developed under my supervision.

These biases can be reduced by training and having higher-level managers review performance appraisals before and after supervisors hold meetings with employees.

One of the most pervasive of all errors in assessing employee performance is the so-called halo effect. This occurs when an employee is judged on the basis of an overall impression that the supervisor gains from certain traits and characteristics observed or thought to have been observed. Based on this partial information, the supervisor develops an overall or gut feeling about the employee. Gut feelings can be accurate, but they are often prone to error because they are based on emotion, not facts.

Overall impressions of employees are more likely to occur when the appraisal is based on: (1) a characteristic or trait that is of moral importance to the supervisor or others; (2) only a few characteristics or traits from which overall conclusions are drawn; (3) the supervisor's inability to properly assess his or her observations; or (4) the influence of others upon a supervisor's judgments.

Closely related to the halo effect are biases that occur when judgment of one performance factor is allowed to spill over into another. For example, because an employee is judged low on attendance, it is only logical that his quantity of work must be low. This may or may not be true. Supervisors, like anyone else who judges someone's performance, can be prone to rationalize or use flawed logic to draw conclusions about behavior. For example, one might conclude that if an employee cannot get along with others, she cannot possibly do a good job. Again, this may be true, but it is not necessarily the case. An employee whose performance is totally dependent upon her own efforts could be a higher performer and not get along with others. On the other hand, if an employee's performance is dependent upon the cooperation of others and she cannot get along with people, her performance would probably suffer accordingly.

An error that is most often observed when appraising the work of a group is the statistically normal distribution error. The performance of the members of a group is usually not evenly distributed—some will perform better than others. A distribution or statistical curve exists. If supervisors can consistently and accurately measure both individual and group performance, then the appraisals will correspond.

Developing Performance Criteria and Standards

It is management's responsibility to determine the criteria upon which performance is judged. The factors or criteria will vary among different types of jobs. For example, demonstrated leadership is an important performance criterion for supervisors, but most likely not a factor for custodians. It is also important that performance factors be weighted—that is, some relative value or importance must be attached to each factor. The purpose of weighting is to help employees understand what areas of job performance are emphasized, and to ensure that supervisors are consistent in ranking or weighting the relative importance of factors.

People want to believe that the ways they behave and how they do their jobs are right. They have a tremendous capacity to rationalize their behavior as correct given particular facts, circumstances, and conditions. In the absence of feedback, employees will likely conclude from their own viewpoints that what they have been doing is right and that they have been doing it well. They expect to get rewarded proportionately for what they view as their contributions. If they are suddenly told that how they have been behaving is wrong, what they have accomplished is unacceptable, and that rewards will not be forthcoming, problems will occur.

When employees internalize that their behavior or job performance is not up to what they perceive as acceptable levels, they will normally be motivated to change. However, once employees conclude that their behavior or job performance is acceptable, most do not continually try to do better.

There are some employees who are what are commonly known as high achievers. They are employees who continually set increasingly challenging goals and higher standards of performance for themselves. The great majority of employees who are not high achievers are influenced by factors that affect their aspirations, goals, needs, and job performance. Peer pressure is one significant factor, for example. Unless supervisors establish and communicate performance standards, employees will be influenced by others to establish their own performance standards. It is not unusual to find that employee standards for what they believe is a good job are lower than the organization's standards or expectations.

Whatever standards or expectations for performance are developed, they must be communicated to employees. Employees must accept these standards as requirements of their jobs. Performance must be judged, feedback given, corrective action taken when necessary, and rewards given to those whose performance meets or exceeds the standards. All of this is more easily stated than properly carried out.

For instance, when people think of standards, their first thought is basic time-motion studies, commonly referred to as stopwatch standards, which often generate negative feelings. Industrial or methods engineers tend to have negative images and arouse insecurity and other emotions whenever they start to time-study jobs. I speak from experience, having worked as an industrial engineer and later supervised industrial engineers. The tensions caused by attempting to time jobs, and the games played by management and employees to bias the standards, often make the effort to establish standards not worth the time or cost. For these reasons, the use of time-study standards has generally declined.

In the past few years there has been some resurrection of time-study. Where is it done today, it is not done with a stopwatch. It is done electronically in jobs where employees do relatively repetitive work using a computer. An example is airline ticket-reservation agents or telephone information operators. Work is electronically monitored to see how many inquiries are handled in specified increments of time. With airline reservation personnel working at a regional reservations center, the number of calls taken and resultant reservations made can be gathered, compiled, and analyzed. From data analysis, standards can be developed.

The use of time-study standards has also declined because of the complexity of jobs in interrelated work environments. In many organizations, jobs are so highly integrated that separating one from another to establish standards is almost impossible. Does this mean that performance standards should not or cannot be established? The answer is no.

Many supervisors, higher-level managers, staff personnel, and employees have argued that standards for jobs cannot be established. Their arguments grow louder as work becomes less repetitive or routine. They say that because many job activities vary widely on a day-to-day basis, it is impossible to obtain or develop meaningful measurements. These arguments lack merit because they are based on an assumption that a precise standard needs to be developed. There is virtually no job where some type of standard or expectation cannot be developed—but the standards do not have to be precise. What is important is that employees have a clear understanding of what is expected of them. All employees develop their own ideas as to what constitutes good or bad performance. All supervisors do the same. The objective is for supervisors and employees to develop similar ideas about good or bad performance.

There are three basic approaches that can be taken to developing standards:

1. Management can create the standards and communicate them to employees. Most often industrial engineers working with supervisors and higher-level managers develop the standards. Employees do not play a significant role in their creation, if they play any role at all. This approach is the one that most organizations have historically used.
2. Employees, individually or in groups, can develop performance criteria. Once developed, they are then communicated to management. If the trend toward employee empowerment continues, this approach will become more commonplace. Historically, few managements have officially sanctioned employees' developing their own performance standards.
3. Collaboration involves supervisors and employees jointly developing performance criteria and standards. It works best when employees are responsible and where management does not feel threatened by employee involvement. It is often borne out of necessity because supervisors often know far less about individual jobs than the incumbent employees know about their work.

Types of Performance Standards

There are many types of standards in any organization. They can range from standards for personal hygiene to standards for quality. The less analysis that goes into developing a standard, the higher the probability that the standard will be inaccurate.

Many standards for job performance are based on history and tradition within an organization. In fact, some organizations communicate their standards for service, product quality, and the like in their motto or logo. For example, the Ford Motor Company has used the statement "Quality Is Job 1" to communicate its standards. The Federal Express motto is: "Absolutely Positively the Best in the Business" to communicate an image. Standards such as these often become a tradition, and employees at all levels are expected to live up to these standards. But slogans and mottos are useful only if each employee understands what it means with respect to his or her job and translates it into actual job performance.

Historical standards, while usually of high value in influencing employee behavior, can have an opposite effect. Some organizations and supervisors do not change standards or adjust to changing needs and conditions. Traditions and past practices verbally expressed as "we have always done it this way," or "it was good enough for me, therefore, it's good enough for you," can impede rather than enhance performance. Historical standards, whether they are organization-wide or unique to a particular group, must be continually assessed. When necessary, they must be changed.

Another class of standards are engineered standards. These standards are usually very precise, developed through careful analysis and measurement. They may be developed through records analyses, as in the case of cost standards, or by use of time studies, as in the case of defining normal output in a given period of time for the average employee. Some jobs more than others lend themselves to precise measurement.

Standards may also be expressed as objectives or goals. An objective, whether to reduce absenteeism, improve quality, or increase profits, is a standard of performance that is to be achieved. Setting objectives and goals gives employees something upon which to focus their efforts. The process commonly known as Management by Objectives (MBO) involves establishing standards of performance or accomplishment that employees are required to attempt to achieve. Contrary to popular opinion, managing by objectives per se is nothing new. People, as individuals and in groups, have been planning and directing their behavior to reach objectives for tens of thousands of years.

A class of standards that often cause problems are the subjective standards: feelings, attitudes, or vague or general statements. All organizations have varieties of subjective standards that may vary widely within the organization. What constitutes good or bad performance in one group can be quite different for another. Standards of dress, etiquette, cooperation, integrity, courtesy, or morality—just to name a few—tend to more subjective than objective. There is nothing wrong with subjective standards per se. Many types of behavior and activities cannot be precisely or sometimes even generally prescribed. The main problem is developing a common understanding of what each standard means. The greater the degree of interpretation, the greater the degree of variance in behavior from the standard. This, of course, often leads to the necessity for corrective action.

Traditionally, standards have been viewed as part of control processes. Standards do serve to establish limits for behavior and performance, which makes them control mechanisms. However, standards should also be used for development purposes. By establishing standards that employees have to strive to reach and maintain, supervisors help employees develop as workers and as human beings. Accomplishment and achievement usually serve to generate feelings of pride, satisfaction, respect, and dignity.

Once standards or expectations are established, they must be communicated. Employee performance, as compared to standards or exceptions, must be judged to determine which employees meet or exceed standards and which do not. Rewards to reinforce desired behavior, and corrective action to influence a change in unacceptable behavior, must correlate with standards or expectations.

Regardless of what performance criteria are used, it is essential for employees to understand the factors on which performance is judged, what these factors actually mean, and just what constitutes the various degrees of performance. Each employee should have a clear understanding of what terms such as *quality of output, work habits, communication skills,* and the like actually mean—what is considered to be above standard and what is below standard performance.

Observing the Efforts

Once job responsibilities, performance factors, and standards are established and understood, supervisors need to learn on a continuing basis how employees are doing with respect to carrying out their job duties. Supervisors rarely have the time to continually monitor employee activities. Even if they did, it would be unwise to continually watch over employees. Few people like to have someone looking over their shoulder unless they are in a crisis and need assistance, or they are in training. Competent, responsible, trustworthy employees should be allowed to do their jobs without being under the continual watchful eye of a supervisor.

But if you're not continually monitoring what employees are doing, how are you to know what they are actually getting done? The answer is that you establish sensors. Sensors are the key things supervisors need to know about what employees are doing. For example, you may need to know if certain work was performed at the end of a week, but you do not need

to know what has been accomplished on a day-to-day basis. In this case, you get feedback at the end of the week. For some types of work, you need to have feedback on how the work is actually being done. By identifying what's important in each job, you can decide what to monitor and how often.

Supervisors are not going to see, hear, or know everything that employees do over a span of time, be it three months or a year. What this means is that the more gaps and voids, the less supervisors can substantiate judgments about performance factors. If gaps exist, then how can a supervisor judge whether performance has exceeded, met, or is below standard? You assign a neutral rating to any performance factor for which little or no information is available. A neutral rating might be "average," "adequate," "meets requirements," "meets standards," or something comparable. If the employee disagrees, then he or she shoulders the burden of proof. The neutral rating is because it is impossible to support a higher or lower rating.

The following example further illustrates this important point. Organizational policy requires that appraisals for all employees be done at a specific designated time. Suppose an employee had been in a unit only for thirty days, and it was time to do the annual performance appraisal. Further, the employee was newly hired from the outside. The supervisor who has to do the appraisal had been out of town for most of those thirty days. So the supervisor has to judge this employee's performance on factors such as productivity, quality, interpersonal relations, and initiative. How should the employee be judged if the performance degrees for each factor are "exceeds standards," "meets standards," "below standards"? The only logical, sensible, and defensible answer is "meets standards." While this is an unusual situation, it makes a point: Whenever there is a substantial absence of information about some aspect of an employee's job performance, give the employee the benefit of the doubt and assign a neutral rating. If there's limited information and it is either highly positive or negative, a higher or lower rating could be assigned with caution. But if the employee, and most likely it would be in the case of a low rating, presents substantial information of a positive nature to fill in the void, then re-examine all the information to determine what is the most accurate to assign.

Record Maintenance—Documentation

When it comes to having substantiable information to support their opinions about employee performance, the great majority of supervisors do a poor job. Too many supervisors simply will not take the time to develop the necessary documentation. If supervisors were told that their own performance appraisal would in part be determined by the accuracy of the appraisals they do, supervisors would most assuredly do a far better job.

If you fail to keep timely and accurate information in writing about each employee's job performance, you fall into one of two possible psychological traps. First is the *primacy effect,* in which people tend to remember the major events in their life. Supervisors, over a year's time, assuming such is the normal appraisal period, will remember the big things that an individual will have done; they will remember both the major good and bad things, although the bad things are likely to be remembered more. When it comes time for the annual performance appraisal, it's those major things that dominate the appraisal. The usual result is something far removed from how the employee performed overall. The second trap is the *recency effect,* in that people usually have better recall of what happened recently than long ago. (An exception can exist for significantly traumatic events.) To test this, ask someone what he had for breakfast on a particular day a month earlier. If you report to someone who is a notoriously bad record keeper, God help you if you screw up on the job the day before your annual performance review. What typically happens is that recent recall overshadows past recall. Of course, this could work in an employee's favor if he did something exceptionally praiseworthy the day before his performance review.

Does record keeping mean you need to follow employees around with pen and paper, making notes? Of course not. But it does mean that periodic notes have to be made. Supervisors keep notes in their heads, anyway; why not make things a bit easier by writing them down so you do not have to continually remember everything? Develop a working file on all employees. This is current data on employees—that is, within the past twelve to eighteen months. (Permanent files are normally kept by the human resources department.) Once a month, or even once every two or three months, make some comments in the working file based on the feedback you have obtained on what employees have accomplished relative to their normal job duties. If no new information has been obtained, or the information indicates employees are meeting normal expectations, no notes need be made. Remember, an absence of information to indicate good or bad performance means a neutral rating should be assigned.

If negative information is noted in the working file, inform the employee in order for him or her to have a timely opportunity to challenge the remarks. Some supervisors feel that time shouldn't be taken out to note the good or normal things employees do; they believe it is only necessary to note the negative things. This means that the best rating any employee could get would be neutral—there would never be anything to substantiate a higher rating. To avoid overloading your computer or file cabinet with out-of-date information, discard the information once the formal appraisal is done and it passes review with the employee and whomever else in the organization is involved in the review process.

The performance appraisal speaks for itself. If an employee disagrees with his or her appraisal, but fails to challenge it in a timely manner through formal channels, the window of opportunity has closed. Remember that when you can support your opinion about job performance with substantive, credible information, you will do a more accurate job of judging performance, be better prepared to support your judgments to all concerned, and if challenged be better prepared to defend your positions. Keep in mind that the primary purpose of performance appraisals is to give employees relatively accurate feedback on their performance; documentation facilitates this purpose.

Providing Feedback

Supervisors must create either formal or informal opportunities to give feedback to employees on their job performance. If employees are doing well and are on track, they should be told so. This affirms that what they have been doing is proper and correct. When you sit down with an employee for a formal performance appraisal, both of you should have a pretty clear notion of what the outcome will be. An appraisal where the employee is either pleasantly surprised because it was far better than he or she expected, or disappointed because it was far worse, could signal a failure to communicate on your part. Recognize also that some employees refuse to listen to messages or heed their content. They act surprised when given a poor appraisal, even though they have received timely feedback throughout the period.

Periodic feedback gives an employee the opportunity to either defend performance or move decisively to self-correct before performance deteriorates further. Feedback can be in any way, shape, or form that you feel is appropriate.

Conducting a Successful Performance Appraisal

Supervisors must view performance appraisal as a primary responsibility, a way to facilitate cooperation and maintain high performance. Performance appraisals must also be viewed as an employee development and counseling tool. High performance must be supported and reinforced by appropriate rewards. Behavior and performance that do not meet expectations must be handled through corrective action and the withholding of rewards. Performance appraisals must be seen as a way to assist employees in developing, so that they can achieve many of the things they aspire to in their career. The following guidelines can be employed in reducing the stress associated with a face-to-face discussion of performance with an employee.

• A performance appraisal is not something you do at the last moment and then hand to the employee. It must be carefully planned. In preparing for a performance appraisal meeting, use all available records so that your opinions are supported by facts.

• The employee's performance for the entire time period—for example, six months or a year—must be considered. Don't overemphasize unusual or isolated incidents that are atypical. Don't be influenced by previous appraisals, either. A change in the level of performance does not necessarily mean that the present or previous appraisal is incorrect. It does suggest, however, that an inquiry be made into the reasons for the change in performance.

• Most performance-appraisals systems identify a number of performance factors—for example, quantity of work, quality of work, cooperation, adaptability, interpersonal relations, work habits, job knowledge, and attendance. Avoid halo effect and spillover errors. Consider each factor as distinct from all other factors. Be careful not to compare one employee with another—employee performance should be compared against standards or expectations, not one against another.

• Don't allow an employee's level or length of service to affect the performance appraisal. An employee with a lot of skill and experience should generally be held to higher standards of performance than an inexperienced employee. Because an employee has been doing a particular job for many years does not necessarily mean that he or she is a higher performer. Nor is it necessarily true than an inexperienced employee will perform at a lower level.

• Don't rush a performance-appraisal meeting. As a guideline, budget forty-five minutes to an hour for a meeting. Keep the meeting private, and keep telephone or other interruptions to an absolute minimum. Don't allow yourself to be influenced by compensation considerations; the employee's need for money, inflation, or the few dollars that have been budgeted for raises should not be considered in the appraisal. Even if there were no money available for raises, performance appraisals should be conducted.

• Don't be afraid to go on record with your opinions about an employee's performance. Performance-appraisal meetings do not always run smoothly. This is especially true when employees are told that their performance is below standards. Some employees are very skillful manipulators and will use emotions, fears, prejudices, intimidation, hostility, and even threats to influence the outcome of their appraisal. If you have prepared for the appraisal meeting, you will likely have anticipated an employee's behavior and should be able to handle any situations that arise.

• During the performance-appraisal meeting, listen to what the employee has to say about his or her appraisal. The employee should be given the opportunity to talk about his or her own perceptions of his or her performance. If a disagreement exists, ask yourself, "Can I support my opinions about this employee's performance?" View the meeting as having a constructive rather than a destructive purpose. If an employee's performance is not up to standards or expectations in any or all areas, it is your responsibility to help the employee to see that behavior and performance need to be changed. If an employee's performance meets or exceeds standards or expectations, that behavior needs to be reinforced by rewards.

Preparing for the Meeting

Restudy the job duties of the employee whose performance is going to be appraised. In light of the employee's duties, performance will be judged against standards, expectations, and applicable goals. Be prepared to support your opinions by citing facts, incidents, situations, and cases. Also give some thought to what you would like to see accomplished in the meeting.

Performance-appraisal forms should not be filled out in ink or typed prior to the meeting. Leave the form blank or fill it out in pencil. The meeting is a two-way process, and before any judgments are finalized you need to review them with the employee. Typing or ink projects an image of finality—and besides, it does not erase well. While a performance-appraisal meeting is not a collective bargaining session, it is wise practice to hear what an employee has to say before results are finalized. Employee input could result in modification of your initial opinions.

What about having employees fill out appraisals on themselves? This isn't a bad idea, since employees have already done so in their minds prior to a meeting. If you employ this practice, simultaneously put your respective appraisals on the desk. If employees are asked to do so first, it is akin to putting the primary responsibility on their shoulders. Also, if employees rate themselves lower than you would, it becomes rather convenient for you to go along with the employee's appraisal and perhaps save a few dollars on a raise. Having employees do written appraisals on themselves for presentation at a performance-appraisal meeting is *not* recommended if feedback on performance has been inadequate or poor relations exist between you and the employees. In such cases, perceptions may be quite different, and putting significantly different appraisals on the table could precipitate a confrontation.

The Time and Place

Appraisal time frames are usually stipulated by organizational policy and procedure. Too many organizations still follow the practice of having all appraisals done at one time—for example, the last week of a calendar year. The problem is that supervisors have many other things to do, and when ten or more appraisals have to be done in one week, the appraisals are likely to get short-changed. It is best to spread them out over the year and do them on each employee's anniversary date of hire.

The performance appraisal should be conducted in your office or a conference room where privacy is ensured. Project the image that the meeting is an important agenda item, not a disagreeable task that needs to be done as quickly as possible.

Conducting the Meeting

It is rather common for supervisors and employees alike to feel anxiety. Anxieties and tensions can be lessened, however. For example, try to act naturally and be courteous to the employee when he arrives. Offer a cup of coffee, tea, or soft drink. If this is an employee's first appraisal, discuss its purpose and objectives. Point out that the purpose is to formalize judgments, help the employee develop, career counsel, determine allocation of rewards, and so on. Stress the positives of performance appraisals. Performance appraisals are only used for corrective or disciplinary action when such becomes necessary.

Discuss each performance factor individually. Review contributions and strengths prior to discussing deficiencies. Support your opinions to the extent realistically possible by citing specific examples. Avoid vagueness and sweeping generalities. Communicate an appreciation for the individual's contributions.

Most performance-appraisal forms have a category titled "employee weaknesses," "areas for improvement," or something akin. There is nothing wrong per se with such a category, but problems do arise when supervisors are required to make some comment. If an employee has serious or potentially serious problems, by all means these should be noted. However, it is unlikely that the majority of employees have such problems. Nobody is perfect, though some supervisors and higher-level managers operate with the serious misconception that it is their responsibility to make employees perfect. Focus on employee strengths and don't dwell on minor deficiencies or faults. In effect, employees need to be accepted, warts and all.

Consider the following: An employee performs the vast majority of his job duties extremely well and exhibits some minor deficiencies. His supervisor judges him an excellent employee, but because the form requires the information, she notes the minor deficiencies. She also notes that the employee is improving on these deficiencies. Now what do you think the employee is going to remember—the 95 percent that was excellent or the 5 percent that was deficient? The latter, of course. The result is that the performance appraisal has been somewhat tainted. Clearly, some deficiencies just should not be mentioned. They are not potentially serious enough to warrant mentioning or attempting to correct.

Now, if potentially serious problems exist, then it is important to clearly point them out to the employee and attempt to get the individual to take corrective action. A problem-solving approach works for most cases. In cases where the employee will not commit to change or has failed to make good on prior commitments, then direct suggestions and even mandates can be given.

After all the performance factors have been discussed, summarize the appraisal. As appropriate, career counseling and discussion of deficiencies should take place. Many organizations have a policy of not allowing supervisors to discuss salary increases in conjunction with performance appraisals: Management does not want performance appraisals and raises linked. Such logic is seriously flawed. The opportunity to get salary increases and other rewards is very important to employees. It is ridiculous for top-level managers making six- and seven-figure incomes to say that money does not motivate employees. (For those who think this way, an easy way to test their convictions is to ask them if they would be willing to do their jobs for half of what they are currently being paid, or if they will forgo raises when good performance has been rendered.) If policy permits, tell employees at

the end of the performance-appraisal meeting what raise is being recommended. The word *recommended* should be emphasized, especially if appraisals and recommended raises are reviewed by higher authority. If you do a
credible job on performance appraisals, then your recommended raises should
be approved.

In concluding a performance-appraisal meeting, you should:

1. Summarize what was discussed during the meeting.
2. Restate what has been mutually agreed upon. Restate areas of disagreement and the reasons for them.
3. When the need for improvement has been discussed, make sure you
   have a clear understanding of the employee's specific intentions, or
   lack thereof, to change behavior.
4. Suggest or schedule follow-up meetings, if advisable.
5. If employees are dissatisfied with the outcome, advise them of their
   rights of appeal, assuming of course that such exist.
6. Always try to end the meeting on a positive note. After the meeting,
   review in your own mind what was accomplished.

10

Employee Counseling

When *counseling* is mentioned, the thought might come to mind of a person being treated by a psychiatrist or psychologist. Psychoanalysis is an effective way of helping people overcome emotional problems, but most behavior problems do not require psychoanalysis. Psychoanalysis requires considerable skill and training, and should never be attempted by supervisors.

For purposes of this book, *counseling* is broadly defined as a communicative relationship between two or more people, whereby one person or a group uses various techniques to help a person help him or herself resolve an existing problem, avoid a potential problem, or make a decision.

Counseling is an implicit part of every supervisor's relationship with employees. All supervisors should receive some minimum training in identifying potential or existing behavior problems. They should also have training in basic techniques and approaches to helping employees help themselves resolve, overcome, or avoid problems. Lastly, supervisors should be able to recognize when an employee's behavior is serious enough to be referred to professional counselors.

It appears that, to a greater degree today than in the past, people are having difficulty dealing with life. Since life at work and outside are inseparable over time, difficulties that employees experience in life can find their way into the work place and affect job performance and relationships. Many people develop strategies to cope with life, and ease their way through personal and work-related problems. However, on occasion even the strongest people need help from others. Some people recognize when they need the help and take necessary steps to obtain it. Others either do not recognize the need or are reluctant to seek help.

Supervisors, whether they like it or not, are often thrust into counseling roles. This is particularly true when the supervisor is someone whom employees respect and trust. An employee may turn to her supervisor—or to a close friend or, in unionized organizations, to the shop steward or committee person. When an employee's behavior problems affect job performance or relationships with others, a supervisor has no choice other than to become involved.

Because supervisors are leaders, employees often look to them for guidance. To some employees, the supervisor is a parent figure. Supervisors who are trusted and respected will find themselves asked for advice and opinions on matters that touch all parts of an employee's life. An untrained supervisor may experience anxiety, apprehension, depression, and even suspicion and fear when he or she is unable or unwilling to counsel an employee who has asked for assistance.

Benefits and Risks of Counseling Employees

Perhaps the most important benefit of becoming involved in employee counseling is that it gives supervisors the opportunity to get to know an employee better and perhaps help another human being. Supervisors who understand how employees think, feel, act, and react are better able to build productive working relationships. Those who take the time to help employees deal with problems find that their prestige and influence increase.

Counseling is beneficial because anxieties are reduced when we get things off our chest. Most employee problems can be resolved or controlled if the individual is able to sort things out and decide on a course of action. Talking things out is an effective way of putting a problem into proper perspective and laying the groundwork for a solution. Because a troubled employee's ego activates defense mechanisms, it is sometimes difficult to face a problem. If employees are unwilling or unable to face their problem, a solution becomes remote. Counseling can stimulate problem-solving behavior. Troubled employees can be influenced to accept the reality of a situation. From there, various approaches to coping with or resolving a problem can be identified and assessed.

Troubled employees are usually dependent upon others to help keep them out of difficulties, or get them out of difficulties they cannot get out of themselves. As long as these employees remain dependent on others, their problems will persist. An important principle of counseling is to teach employees to help themselves; if counseling is successful, it helps employees develop a sense of responsibility.

While the benefits to employees are significant, counseling is not without its risks and dangers; it is somewhat like opening a box the contents of which are unknown. What may appear to be a minor problem may turn out to be the tip of deep-seated emotional illness or character disorder requiring professional assistance. A supervisor who tries to treat an employee with severe psychological or social problems usually ends doing more harm than good. Counseling takes time; a supervisor who has fifteen or more employees may find that he or she cannot afford to take time away from other work to counsel employees. This can be especially true in a high-productivity work environment.

For these two reasons, never attempt to treat an employee who has a serious emotional problem or character disorder. Recognize the possible seriousness of a problem and see to it the troubled employee is referred to experts in human problems for treatment. Make a referral even if you only suspect that a problem is potentially serious. It is better to be safe than sorry. Referral should first be made to higher-level managers or staff experts before a recommendation to seek professional help outside of the organization.

Another risk in counseling employees is inherent in the supervisor-employee relationship: It is virtually impossible for a supervisor to counsel an employee with complete, detached professionalism. The supervisor shares the employee's problem if it is having an effect on job performance. And even under the best conditions, it is difficult for employees to be totally open with supervisors—supervisors are authority figures and their decisions affect the welfare of employees. Employees will always experience some anxiety, apprehension, suspicion, and even fear when discussing problems with a supervisor. This is especially true when sensitive or confidential matters are discussed.

A supervisor's knowing highly sensitive or confidential information about an employee could consciously, or unconsciously, affect his or her feelings about the employee. It's the same for adverse information about an employee's health, marital relations, or moral character. For example, even though epilepsy is usually controllable with medication, a social and psychological stigma is often attached to a person with this condition. A supervisor may consciously or unconsciously find reasons to reject for a promotion a qualified employee who has epilepsy.

Another problem associated with counseling employees is the personal relationships that may exist. Familiarity can and occasionally does affect objectivity. On the other hand, an employee's perception of the ability of a supervisor to act as a counselor may be either negatively or positively affected by familiarity. To some employees, the supervisor is a person who is all-knowing and all-seeing. To others, the supervisor is just another person who possesses and exhibits all of the faults and weaknesses associated with human nature.

Recognizing Emotional Illness in Employees

In general, any significant change in an employee's behavior within a relatively short period is cause for concern. When people are confronted with problems and pressures that seem insurmountable, strong feelings of anxiety or guilt may evolve. That part of the human mind called the ego cannot operate properly under anxiety, guilt, or other pressures. To protect itself against these pressures, the ego activates defense mechanisms, either conscious or unconscious. In effect, when people are confronted with pressures they cannot handle, they call upon their defense mechanisms to protect themselves from psychological injury.

Emotional illness is characterized by employees' consciously or unconsciously using defense mechanisms. What differentiates so-called normal from emotionally ill people is the degree to which the defense mechanisms are used. With the exception of sublimation, all emotional illnesses or character disorders are characterized by an abnormal use of one or more of the following defense mechanisms.

• *Repression.* Repression is the underlying basis of all defense mechanisms. Through repression, people keep threatening desires, wishes, fantasies, feelings, and memories in their unconscious. If repressed feelings and thoughts move to the conscious part of the mind, the ego exerts energy to push it back into the unconscious. For example, if something derogatory is said about someone a person greatly admires, that person may pretend not to hear. All supervisors have seen employees selectively hear what they want to hear or see what they want to see. Pretending not to hear or see something that actually occurred is evidence of repression.

• *Rationalization.* Rationalization is the process by which a person imagines or substitutes acceptable reasons for doing something that are altogether different from the real reasons. For example, an employee may rationalize that her reason for working so hard is to be a better provider for her family, when the real reason is that she works for self-fulfillment. Phrases like "I am doing this for my family," or "I am doing this for my company," or "I am doing this for your benefit and not my own" are commonly heard.

• *Sublimination.* Sublimination is the process whereby an unacceptable behavior is channeled into an acceptable behavior. The drive or desire to say or do something that would be socially unacceptable is channeled into a socially acceptable outlet. As an example, a person with a strong desire to commit acts of violence may become a football player. By subliminating, people can be very creative and effective while releasing a potentially destructive drive.

• *Projection.* Projection is the mechanism by which a person's ego transfers to someone else something it cannot accept. For example, a person may not trust himself or herself and may be unable to accept this; in order to avoid the tension and anxiety of having to handle this knowledge, the person will project it onto others by saying that no one can be trusted.

• *Displacement.* Displacement is the process by which a part may come to symbolize the whole, or vice versa. As an example, a person who had a bad relationship with an obese supervisor may exhibit negative feelings about all supervisors who happen to be significantly overweight.

• *Identification.* Identification is the process by which an unacceptable feeling or belief may be made acceptable by identifying it in someone else who personifies it. For example, a person who has a strong prejudice against blacks will not openly express her prejudice, but will identify strongly with someone who openly professes the same prejudice.

• *Regression.* Regression is the process by which people withdraw from a situation they cannot cope with to a situation they can manage. For example, a person may regress into childish behavior which, from his or her perspective, makes him or her better able to deal with situations and events. In extreme form, people can withdraw in a fantasy world and be completely detached from reality.

• *Self-punishment.* In conflict and stress situations, it is not unusual for people to want to inflict some degree of pain and suffering on someone else. If a person cannot bring himself or herself to inflict some injury on the intended recipient, he or she inflicts the injury upon himself or herself.

• *Reaction formation.* Reaction formation is the defense mechanism whereby an undesirable feeling or impulse is kept in the unconscious by strong emphasis on its opposite. For example, a person may intensely dislike the supervisor, but be very friendly toward him or her.

• *Substitution.* Substitution is the process whereby something that is desired or highly valued, which cannot be possessed for psychological reasons, is unconsciously replaced by something that can be possessed and is psychologically acceptable.

• *Fantasy.* Fantasy is the defense mechanism in which a person constructs something in his or her mind that he or she cannot have or experience in reality. For example a person may have a desire to be a neurosurgeon. Since he or she cannot achieve his or her goal, he or she fantasizes that he or she is one.

• *Conversion.* Conversion is the process by which a person converts a psychological conflict into a physical symptom. For example, a person may be afraid of having to do a new job and subsequently develops a physical problem to avoid doing it. Also, an employee may develop a headache or stomachache when his or her problem is that he or she is worried about failing an upcoming job-proficiency test.

• *Compensation.* This is the process whereby a person who has a physical impairment or psychological deficiency emphasizes some other activity or behavior that serves to compensate for the limitation. For example, a person confined to a wheelchair may compensate for the physical limitation by intellectual achievement.

• *Denial.* Denial is the defense mechanism in which the ego refuses to accept, or severely distorts, something that is obvious. As an example, a person who has been denied a promotion may continue to believe that the promotion notice is delayed because of a paperwork backlog or has been lost in the mail.

As people increasingly use these defense mechanisms, their behavior or emotional illness in a mild form is known as *neurosis.* Abnormal behavior or emotional illness in extreme forms is known as *psychosis.* Neurotic behavior is often observed in the form of anxiety (which embodies feelings like tension, uneasiness, distress, and frustration), phobias, obsessions, compulsions, mild depression, extreme fatigue, and hypochondria. Psychosis, referred to as a character disorder, is observed in the form of schizophrenia, paranoia, obsessive-compulsiveness, manic-depressive behavior, masochism, and extreme antisocial behavior. Character disorders appear to be in part inherited and in part due to environmental factors. Character disorders that are caused in part or totally by chemical imbalances or genetic abnormalities cannot be successfully treated by counseling. Neuroses and environmentally caused psychoses can be treated by counseling.

Considering the complexity of human behavior, and the obvious limitations of a supervisor's ability to help employees, employee counseling must be approached with caution. As noted earlier, whether they want to or not, supervisors must be involved in counseling employees with problems that are affecting job performance. For obvious reasons, they should use only the most basic approaches to counseling.

The Counseling Framework

When listening is absent, counseling becomes directive and one-sided. Even if it is decided the employee should be directed to a solution, listening to the employee's reaction is necessary to know whether it is accepted. There is no point in making the effort if the employee has obviously rejected the advice and directions. The employee cannot be forced to change behavior. He or she has the choice and must recognize the potential benefits and costs associated with any decision.

Implicit to counseling is the willingness and ability to *empathize* with the employee. Empathy should not be confused with sympathy or agreement. In empathizing you seek to understand the employee's feelings. If you can see things from the employee's viewpoint, you are likely to establish rapport. After rapport is established, communication is likely to be more free-flowing. Rapport involves three elements: (1) an understanding supervisor, (2) a physical and psychologically nonthreatening climate, and (3) an employee who is willing to accept counseling.

Counseling of personal problems must be conducted in an atmosphere of confidence. Only in exceptional cases, such as that of a seriously maladjusted person, are confidences revealed. For example, confidence should be broken in the case of an employee who carries a firearm and is predisposed to violence, or an employee with strong sexual perversions who works with children. In such cases, more harm could be done if the maladjusted person is allowed to continue functioning in an environment where there is considerable risk to others.

Good listening habits are critical to success, and perhaps the most important element in listening is patience. For many reasons, most people do not come straight to the point when they converse. They meander about until they get the confidence or find the right moment to say what they really want to. A good listener waits to see where the conversation is going before deciding whether and how to influence its course. Most people can work their way through a problem if they just have someone who is willing to listen to them.

Approaches to Counseling

Communication is inherent to counseling, and how a supervisor communicates is inherent to his or her style of managing. For example, the controlling type of supervisor will have a directive style of counseling. A participative type of supervisor will be more receptive to other viewpoints, and be likely to employ a nondirective approach to counseling. Supervisors who function as caretakers rather than managers are inclined to avoid responsibility; their style of counseling is likely to be one of avoidance as well.

The many approaches to counseling range from highly directive to totally nondirective. Basically, the more directive approaches are characterized by giving advice, asking questions, making a diagnosis, and providing answers and solutions. The nondirective approach focuses on the employee's discovering the cause of difficulties and deciding on the proper course of action. The supervisor refrains from giving advice, making a diagnosis, and imposing solutions.

No single approach fits all situations. Each supervisor will eventually use the methods he or she is most comfortable using. Before deciding on the initial approach, however, consider the following:

1. The employee's personality and attitude.
2. The nature of the problem.
3. The seriousness of the situation.
4. The amount of time you are willing to give to counseling.
5. The organization's support system.
6. The degree of success experienced with other employees in taking a particular approach to counseling.

With the basically responsible employee, the approach that appears best suited for most situations is the nondirective or client-centered. The difficult employee or the employee who really needs advice will probably respond better to directive approaches.

The Nondirective Approach

The nondirective or client-centered approach to counseling is different from advice giving and other diagnostic methods because the counselor does not direct the employee's behavior or even give advice as to how to behave. The person is counseled to discover his or her problems himself or herself and work out a solution that fits his or her value system and therefore is acceptable to him or her. The nondirective approach is a good one for supervisors because it avoids making a diagnosis and also the problems associated with making an incorrect diagnosis.

When you engage in nondirective counseling, make it clear that you have a genuine interest in the employee's welfare and development. Recognize the importance of counseling as part of your job responsibilities, but accept your limitations and do not attempt to be a psychoanalyst. As a counselor, accept or tolerate the employee's different values and attitudes and try not to pass judgment on those values. Also help employees to accept responsibility for their own behavior and realize that they are capable of helping themselves cope with or resolve their problems in ways that conform to their own values, beliefs, feelings, and attitudes.

Nondirective counseling requires you to develop effective listening skills, which for many supervisors is not easy. This can be especially true for supervisors who have strong personalities and who are outgoing and assertive. Listening is more than refraining from speaking. Effective listeners avoid showing anger, surprise, joy, sympathy, agreement, or disagreement with whatever employees say. You must also accept or at least tolerate the employee's values and attitudes and try to avoid passing judgment on them. Acceptance should not be confused with agreement or approval.

You must also feel that the employee really wants to do the right thing and can resolve the problems once interfering obstacles are removed. Let the employee work out a solution that is consistent with or conforms to his or her values and beliefs. Of course, any solution must conform with the organization's accepted practices and standards of conduct. In this respect the employee cannot be allowed to carry out off-the-wall solutions. If the aforementioned conditions cannot be met, reconsider using the nondirective approach. Also, if the employee is known to be untrustworthy, irresponsible, immature, or incompetent, reconsider nondirective counseling.

Be as nonjudgmental as possible, because the basic objective of nondirective counseling is to help employees help themselves. Avoiding making judgments does not mean that you cannot inform an emotionally ill employee who asks for certain information; information should be given, unless the employee is seeking the kind of thing that will reinforce his or her own view.

In nondirective counseling, proper interviewing is essential to achieve the best possible results. The employee must feel at ease. The time and place of the meeting are important and should be convenient for both parties. Creating a friendly, nonthreatening environment is important. Pay attention to seating arrangement, lighting, spatial distance, and timing. If the meeting is to be held in the supervisor's office, avoid sitting behind your desk; the desk establishes an unequal and judgmental climate and inhibits communication. A conference room or even the lunch room, if there is privacy, is more appropriate.

It goes without saying that confidences should be maintained. Because a supervisor is an authority figure, it is difficult even under the best of conditions for employees to express their true feelings. Use considerable discretion in handling sensitive or confidential information. Sometimes a problem or the solution to the problem may involve other employees. When this is the case, discuss possible courses of action with the employee before taking action, so as to avoid any possibility of betraying confidences.

In the counseling meeting, attempt to get the employee to speak openly. The room setting and time of meeting help, but the essential ingredient is your communication skill. Questions that call for a yes or no answer tend to reduce the flow of conversation. Questions like "Would you like to discuss it with me?" and "Would you help me better understand your feelings?" encourage expression.

Many employees have difficulty verbalizing their problems. Avoid putting words in the employee's mouth. The nondirective response of "I see" or "I understand" can help encourage the expression of feelings. It is not unusual for gaps of silence to occur, particularly when the employee is thinking or anticipating your reaction. Though you may feel pressured to say something, let the employee restart the conversation. Only initiate conversation if the meeting is in danger of collapsing because of the stress and strain buildup during the silence. In general, when silence lasts longer than ten seconds, which to an inexperienced supervisor could seem like an eternity, it is time to say, "Tell me more."

Experienced supervisors recognize that what employees complain about is often not what is really bothering them. The same can be true in counseling. An employee may talk about a variety of things causing concern or frustration, and her remarks may even be contradictory. It may take some time before the real problems can be identified and discussed.

As part of the nondirective technique, learn how to reflect upon what the employee says. Though some people believe that the nondirective approach means remaining passive, this is incorrect. To be productive, any discussion requires give-and-take. Though the employee should do most of the talking, you must contribute to the discussion. Instead of giving advice, reflect on what the employee has said in order to understand what he or she really means.

This method requires serving as a mirror, restating the key things said by the employee. Key feelings must be reflected so they can be reviewed, discussed, and analyzed. In reflecting key feelings, you allow nonessential information to fall by the wayside. For example, an employee may give all kinds of reasons for believing that he has been treated unfairly. You would reflect on the reasons by restating the key point—that is, the employee's belief that he has been treated unfairly. In reflecting, you avoid using the employee's exact words, phrasing a question or drawing a conclusion. If the employee believes that he has been unfairly denied a raise, you should state, "You feel that you have been treated unfairly." This is a statement of what you believe to be the employee's feeling, not a question or a judgment. In reflecting these feelings, it is also important to be certain the feeling actually expressed is the one reflected. If you attempt to diagnose or anticipate the employee's feelings, the counseling relationship may be damaged.

In counseling it is not unusual for an employee to communicate mixed feelings or make contradictory statements. Rather than point out the inconsistencies, attempt to understand the reasons for them. Ask the employee to restate what has been said, to clarify feelings and understandings.

If an employee becomes emotional during the counseling, let her work through these emotions. Direct involvement is necessary only if the employee gets very depressed, hysterical, or enraged. After an emotional release, the employee may feel shame or guilt. If the employee wants to discuss the matter, he or she should be allowed to talk about it.

When an employee displays feeling of confusion, hostility, insecurity, fear, or rejection, reflect on possible solutions or courses of action brought out during the conversation. Exercise care to avoid pushing the employee toward a course of action he or she may not be ready to accept. Remember, the objective of nondirective counseling is for the employee, rather than the supervisor, to develop a solution to the problem.

Giving Advice

As an approach to counseling, giving advice can be useful. Many problems that employees face are relatively simple, and advice can save time and energy and enhance relationships. Obviously, giving advice as a form of counseling should not be considered when you suspect that the employee has an emotional illness or character disorder.

The employee should know that the advice come from your perspective and experience, and that it may or may not fit the employee's situation and values. The employee must also understand that he or she alone must decide whether to accept or reject the advice. If this precaution is not taken, the employee may misinterpret your intentions. Many a supervisor has given advice with the best of intentions, only to have it backfire. Advice should be given only after it is felt that the employee is genuinely seeking it and is able to properly assess it. The more serious and personal the employee's problem, the more cautious you should be about giving advice.

Supervisors who are asked for advice should preface their comments with statements like "From my experience," "The way I view the situation," or "If I were in your situation, I would consider." Such prefatory remarks help the employee understand that the advice is given from the supervisor's perspective.

In giving advice, be careful to avoid diagnosing an employee's problem and recommending a solution that, from the your perspective, will resolve the problem. The wrong problem may be identified, and the solution may not fit the employee's value system. In addition, the employee may be unable to carry out the recommended course of action. Finally, the recommended course of action may turn out to be entirely wrong and produce disastrous results. In summary, give advice to employees only when sincerely requested—and always give it with caution.

Counseling's Relationship to Employee Job Status

Supervisors, higher-level managers, and staff professionals recognize that employees will experience legitimate physical, psychological, or social problems at some point in their lives. It is also well accepted that employees are valuable assets and are long-term investments. Every supervisor who becomes involved in counseling an employee with serious problems comes face-to-face with the question: "To what extent should the employee's situation affect his job status?"

There are no set formulas or easy answers to this question. A lot depends upon past and prevailing practices, the quality and length of the employee's service, past performance, potential, and the extent to which the problem persists or may reoccur.

When a decision must be made regarding the job status of an employee with serious legitimate physical or mental problems, seek the advice and counsel of higher-level managers and staff professionals. As a guide, if the problem is seriously affecting a person's job performance or relationships with others, in addition to receiving counseling, the employee should be considered for a medical leave. This leave should be considered if the employee's record warrants that she has earned one, and that it will help the employee overcome or control her problem.

Although the employee's employment is secure for the duration of the leave, raises and promotion may not be forthcoming, because she is not performing the job and therefore has not earned a raise or promotion. If the problem cannot be overcome, depending upon the facts and circumstances pertaining to the case, the employee should be placed on permanent disability, transferred to a position where she can make a contribution, be subject to disciplinary action up to and including suspension with the intent to discharge, or be retired.

While organizations must be sensitive and compassionate toward employee problems, no business organization is a social welfare agency. Employers and employees alike pay taxes to support government social agencies and social programs. Business organizations have an overriding obligation and responsibility to survive and prosper in order to serve society's needs effectively and efficiently. To this end, employees must understand that no matter how real their problems are, there is some point at which the organization can no longer retain them if they are consistently unable to meet minimum job requirements.

11

Time and Stress Management

Time is certainly one of life's most precious commodities. If a person lives to be eighty years old, he or she will have been alive for a scant 29,200 days. This amounts to only 700,800 hours, of which roughly one-third are spent sleeping. As has so often been said: "So little time, and so much to do." As the pace of life has accelerated and its complexity increased, most people find themselves with more and more demands placed on their time. Because of responsibilities and obligations, many people find that much of their time really isn't their own.

The clock on the wall or the watch on the wrist is the key machine that has and continues to dominate our culture. In a strange sort of way, the clock is like a deity directing our lives. We get up, eat, work, sleep, and even relax by the clock. Two important questions you need to answer are: (1) How much time do you really have control over? and (2) How well do you manage the time that you do control?

One component for achieving success is learning how to effectively use time. *Time management* is something of a misnomer. We cannot manage time; the clock moves at a constant rate. What people can do is develop habits that enable them to get more accomplished in the time available to them. Peoples' lives are shaped by the habits of others and their own habits. People form habits, and habits form futures. It is important that these habits work for people, and not against them. People can only change by changing their habits, since it is habits that cue behavior. Effective managers of time have learned how to make time count. They have learned how to efficiently plan, organize, use, and control their own time and to a degree the time of others. In effect, time management is activity management.

Always keep in mind that better time management enables people to become more efficient. Without goals and objectives to work toward, people will not be effective. Better use of time is a process, or a means to achieving certain ends, not an end in itself.

Time management is important not only on the job but in every aspect of living. The first step in learning how to better manage time is to analyze how it is used. As a supervisor, you must also study how to manage the time of others, and how others with whom they interact manage their time. In a world where people are to varying degrees dependent upon one another, how others manage their time can greatly affect how we manage ours. Whether waiting for a slow clerk at a checkout counter or for someone to complete a task before you can start yours, other people's wasted time affects your time as well.

Obstacles to Controlling Our Lives

Both on and off the job people find there are many obstacles to controlling their lives. Some obstacles are ones people truly have no control over, while others are ones they think they have no control over, but in reality they could control. So often, people convince themselves they have to do certain things, but if they scrutinized these activities they would find the obligations were self-imposed. A person may feel she has to take a child to the local shopping mall and then pick the child up because the child has voiced such a desire, and has gone so far as to imply that the parent is unfair in denying the request. The parent really does not have to take the child, especially if she has a backlog of things to do. However, out of a sense of duty, possibly guilt, or even just to get the child to stop nagging, the parent gives in. People need to consider their priorities, options, and alternatives before allowing their time to be committed.

On the job, a supervisor may believe he must continue attending a meeting that past attendance has proved to be of no value. A supervisor may continue receiving reports because she may miss something, despite the fact the reports are rarely read and nothing useful has even come of the ones that have been read. Too often, supervisors continue to habitually do things that end up being a waste of time. Instead of re-assessing how their time is used, and determining how much of what they do actually contributes to efficiently and effectively meeting goals, they adhere to bad habits. Remember that as goals and priorities change, you must re-assess how your time is used.

Because the pace of life has accelerated, people often find themselves continually running a marathon. It comes down to: Run here, there, everywhere; do this, that, everything. People need to stop and think about what is truly important to them in life. They must also decide what purposes are being fulfilled and what benefits are being derived in their lives. People should also recognize that they are continually bombarded with advertising messages that stress the need to conform while simultaneously preaching the gospel of individuality. For example: An advertisement for a perfume may project the concept of uniqueness for the person using that particular brand. In reality, the more people follow advertisers' messages and eat certain foods, wear certain clothes, and drive certain types of cars, the more they become alike.

One of the greatest obstacles to controlling our lives is procrastination. People are inclined to do what makes them comfortable and happy, and avoid that which makes them uncomfortable and unhappy. They will often spend more time and energy avoiding a task than it takes to accomplish it. As has often been said, procrastination is the great thief of time.

People will often talk about the need to change behavior, but will not take the initiative to change. Seminars, books, cassettes, and videotapes on time management have been in vogue. Most of what these authors say is correct and applicable, however the time many people spend listening and reading about time management is itself a waste of time. Why? Because most people do not internalize the message, commit to putting the ideas into practice, and then assess what was achieved. Many make feeble attempts, but when doing so causes discomfort, they abandon the efforts and revert to old time-wasting habits.

Common Time Wasters

The following identifies many common time wasters. How many do you do? (This list is not inclusive, by any means):

- Scheduling too much time for a task. Work can and often does expand to fill the time available.
- Being overwhelmed by the amount of work and the conflicting demands. This causes stress and strain, which in turn causes a person to develop defense mechanisms that can lead to further waste of time.
- Procrastinating when they do not like or want to do certain things.
- Being afraid of losing control, or fearing some job will not be done right if someone else does it. These are two of the biggest reasons

for a supervisor's failure to delegate. Trying to do everything yourself often wastes time because you have no time to manage.

- Lacking plans, objectives, goals, and priorities for a daily, weekly, monthly, and longer period. People without a sense of direction or purpose waste time.
- Having poorly defined or ambiguous plans, goals, objectives, priorities.
- Poorly organizing your thoughts and activities. Poor organization often displays itself as sloppiness. Having things in their proper place and having a proper place for everything is important. Well-organized people know where things are, and do not waste time looking for them. A well-organized person projects an image of efficiency.
- Fearing loss of status, prestige, and even your job. Some people create unnecessary work and activities in order to look busy. They fear that if they do not look busy by coming in to work early, working into the lunch hour, or taking work home they will lose prestige. All organizations have employees who play these games.
- Lacking ability to say no. Some people just cannot bring themselves to say no. This happens whether they are dealing with a spouse, children, friends, salespersons, bosses, peers, or employees.
- Having poor habits. Human beings, to a degree, are creatures of habit. Many of people's daily activities are built around patterns and habits. As goals and priorities change, habits should also change.
- Allowing too many interruptions. Most people allow themselves to be interrupted too easily. Throughout the day, someone tries to use our time for their benefit. Unless people understand their needs, goals, and priorities, they are prone to unnecessary interruptions. In general, the more important or influential a person is, the more people will try to infringe upon his or her time. The telephone is a very useful instrument for communicating, but it is a major source of interruptions. Keeping your door open all the time is also a time waster. There are times when the door should be closed and even locked.
- Doing too much socializing. Socializing is an important aspect of people's lives, however a person's inability to terminate a discussion, telephone call, or a meeting usually leads to a waste of time.
- Receiving and reading unnecessary mail. Some people have to be on every mailing list, both on and off the job. To some, receiving a lot of mail or being on information distribution lists is a source of prestige and status. Taking the time to read all this unimportant mail wastes time.

- Attending unnecessary meetings. Meetings on the job are a fact of life. While some are essential, many are unnecessary. What is even worse is the time wasted in important meetings because of political gamesmanship by participants.
- Being a poor reader. As has been shown consistently by tests and observations, most people are poor readers. A poor reader wastes time because he or she reads slowly and is slow to comprehend what has been read.
- Failing to measure and assess how time is spent. Unless people have feedback to see how effectively their time has been used, it is difficult to know whether present behavior should be continued or changed.
- Being indecisive. Some people never have enough information on which to make a decision, and consequently end up not making any decisions. Others fear being wrong and attempt to avoid mistakes by not making decisions. Both waste time.
- Being distracted by details. It wastes time to attend to details that could be handled by others or should be disregarded.

Determine the extent to which you misuse time by reviewing your daily activities. The best way to solve or overcome any problem is to first identify the underlying causes.

Overcoming Time Management Problems

When analyzing something in an attempt to judge whether it is good or bad, reference points or standards are necessary. Without reference points, it is impossible to make meaningful comparisons. To analyze your use of time, ask these questions:

- Am I doing it in a way that I think is the best?
- Am I using the time to get what I think are the best results?
- Should I change?
- If yes, how should I change?
- Should someone else do it?
- Should it be done at all?
- Should it be done at another time, or in another place?

To facilitate analysis of time use, maintain a log of daily activities, noting time spent doing each. The time log should cover a normal two- to three-day period. It can then be analyzed and evaluated in relation to goals, standards, and priorities. Identify the activities and events that cause time to be wasted. Also identify those activities and obligations that are required and cannot be changed. The latter are the foundation around which other activities are worked.

Planning

The first step in better managing your time is to become time conscious. Time-conscious supervisors are continually sensitive as to how well their time, as well as the time of others, is used. Develop a daily plan or things-to-do list, recognizing the fact that not everything always goes according to plan. Depending upon the type of work you supervise, also require employees to develop and use daily plans.

A daily plan does not have to be an elaborate minute-by-minute schedule; it can be as simple as a list of what needs to be done that day. Once planned activities are listed, compare them to your goals and priorities and change planned activities to concentrate on meeting goals. The final plan should serve as a guide for the day's activities.

The next step in using a daily plan is to organize the day's activities in some type of logical sequence, and to estimate the amount of time for each activity. The organization of activities into logical groups always results in increased efficiency. For example, most people spend Saturdays making trips to the supermarket, drugstore, bank, gas station, hardware store, or discount store. Making a list of what needs to be purchased at each store and arranging the trips in a logical sequence results not only in saving time but also money. Time is saved because duplication is eliminated, and money is saved by reducing the use of the automobile and by purchasing only what is on a list. Studies have shown that shoppers who stick to shopping lists spend less money than those who shop without lists and buy on impulse.

As the day progresses, compare the planned activities to what is being accomplished. Add new activities and delete others. At the end of each day, compare the plan to what was accomplished. Analyze why certain activities were not accomplished. This feedback increases your awareness about the use of time and facilitates planning and organization. Whatever was not accomplished one day becomes a priority item for the next day. Improvement goals should also be established.

Supervisors who plan their activities to meet objectives and stick as close as possible to the daily plan accomplish more in less time. They also accomplish it better. The more accurate you are about your needs, goals, and priorities, the more you can accurately plan and schedule your activities. The more accurate the plan, the less you will be compelled to deviate from it.

Organization

Supervisors who plan ahead also learn to become better organized. Planning and organization go hand in hand. A word of caution about organization is in order. Some people are so highly organized that they become compulsive. Overorganized people can become so structured that they are unable to adjust or adapt to changing conditions. Extremes of any type of behavior can be dangerous.

It is difficult to describe an optimum level of organization or planning; the important thing is to make better use of time. It is also important to remember that the best plan is worthless if it is not followed.

Organization of information is important. Supervisors are required to maintain all types of records. Reference to records and other types of information occurs daily. Developing a classification system and maintaining records in a timely and orderly manner are effective ways to reduce time spent looking for information. A little time spent each day or week on keeping records up to date and discarding information that is no longer needed will pay high dividends.

Supervisors should become adept at using the wastepaper basket. What is not currently needed or will not be needed in the future should be thrown away. The wastepaper basket is very handy to have around when reading mail, memorandums, and other forms of written information.

Establishing and Communicating Priorities

Supervisors in particular are subject to many demands on their time, and it is not unusual for some of the demands to be conflicting. Stress can facilitate achievement or it can destroy life. One of the keys to successful stress management is to direct the stress into productive activity.

Prioritize the demands upon your time. Communicate these priorities to others. This can reduce conflicts in demands and help others understand why their requests cannot always be met when they expect them to be met. Agreement may not always occur, of course. However, communicating priorities is far better than having people develop their own conclusions.

Dictating Equipment

To facilitate the use of time, supervisors should learn how to use dictating equipment. Pocket dictators are relatively inexpensive and pay for themselves almost immediately. Use of dictating equipment, aside from saving time by not writing, pays an added dividend: Dictation requires planning and organizing thoughts and words. Microcassette recorders are also very useful in making a record of certain thoughts. Creativity does not always occur on the job; creative ideas can come at any time of the day, and they often come when they are least expected. Unless the idea is captured on tape or paper, it is apt to be lost; the recorder solves this problem.,

Supervisors in factories and large stores are usually on their feet most of the day. As they tour the plant, warehouse, or store, they either observe things or have things brought to their attention by others. It is difficult to remember everything that is seen or heard. What often happens is that by the time the supervisor gets back to the office, what was observed or heard is partically or entirely forgotten. Again, use of a pocket recorder can eliminate this problem. A small note pad or even index cards are good substitutes for a recorder.

Controlling Interruptions and Socializing

Interruptions are a fact of life and cannot be eliminated, however they can be controlled. Staying busy is a good way to reduce interruptions, since people are less inclined to interrupt someone who is busy. Closing the office door, and even locking it at certain times, can be very effective in reducing interruptions.

In any social situation, two or more people's time is involved. The central time-management question is: Who is controlling whose time? On the job, supervisors should interact with employees. It is better to visit employees at their work areas rather than have them come to visit you, because it is easier for you to walk away from a conversation. When an employee is in your office, it is not so easy to walk away or terminate a conversation.

This guideline does not always apply, of course. For many reasons, especially if discipline is involved, you may want the employee to come to your office. Also, while more skill is required, it is possible to control socializing when an employee is in your office. Remember the purpose of the visit; once the objective is achieved, continued socializing is unnecessary.

When employees or others socialize with you, let them know how much time you have available. Exercise caution in telling others how much of your time they can use. However, rudeness, abruptness, or aggressiveness can impede communication. Tact and diplomacy should be the guiding principles. Letting others know that you have to attend a meeting, keep another appointment, make some telephone calls, complete some reports, or even go to the bathroom can be effective ways to terminate a social visit without being rude or abrupt.

Time spent socializing can also be reduced if a stand-up meeting is held. If a visitor sits in a comfortable chair, he or she can become glued to it. This can be especially true when employees have to stand at their jobs or work in somewhat unpleasant conditions. Employees can easily stretch a work break by coming into the supervisor's office and talking while sitting in a comfortable chair. In factories, employees often go to their supervisor's air-conditioned office and socialize just to get away from the heat and noise on the floor. Under these conditions, employees sitting in comfortable chairs in an air-conditioned office will always prolong a conversation. Carrying on a discussion while standing almost always reduces this time.

Some people will come into your office and say they only want a minute of your time. If no time can be spared, tactfully but firmly say so, and if appropriate, schedule a time to meet. Another approach is to tell the person that a minute or two is all you can give. If they continue beyond the alloted time, politely end the interaction. If they asked for just a couple of minutes and then take more of your time, they have broken their word and you needn't feel guilty about stopping the person. This is a very effective technique for dealing with salespeople who often say they just want a minute of your time, but in reality want much, much longer.

Managing Telephone Calls

Few supervisors have the luxury of a personal secretary who can screen visitors or telephone calls. Higher-level managers generally have secretaries, but often do not always use them properly. The key to managing telephone conversations lies in how the conversation starts. Questions about the weather, sports, politics, or the caller's health will always lengthen the call. Conversations should be kept to the purpose of the call. If a caller wants to talk about the weather, politics, or sports, advise the person that you need to know specifically what is wanted in order to help them.

Telephone tag is another time-wasting problem supervisors encounter. This is when a person calls and you are out of the office. You return the call, only to find the person whom you called is out of the office. This goes on and on until one party finally makes direct contact with the other. Electronic voice mail systems and portable telephones have significantly reduced telephone tag. If such tools are not available, consider asking what the best time is to reach the person whom you are trying to contact, or via a third party taking a message as to when you can be reached.

Managing Mail

Junk mail is not only received at home. Most organizations generate too much information, be it paper or electronic. Large organizations in particular tend to bureaucratize themselves by generating too much information. To avoid having to handle unnecessary information, get off the mailing or distribution lists. Next, learn to distinguish between important and unimportant mail. Although it may be difficult to track down the source selling your name for home mail, it is easier to do on the job. Learn how to screen mail. When it is addressed to occupant or has a mailing label affixed, it is usually less important than mail that is personally addressed. Looking at the return address to see who sent the mail facilitates screening.

Screen your mail by reading the first couple of paragraphs of a letter and quickly scanning the rest. If the first few paragraphs appear unimportant, immediately discard it. If in doubt, read further and then decide whether the letter requires action.

Improving Reading and Writing Skills

The nation's educational systems have failed to teach people how to read. As a result, many people are slow readers. If this is your problem, take steps to correct it. Popularly advertised speed-reading courses can be helpful, but not essential. Continuing education courses in high schools and colleges or practicing reading can help significantly.

Consonant with improved reading skills is improved writing skills. Poor readers are often poor writers. Good writing requires planning and organization. Many good books and courses are available to help you improve your writing; the time and money spent will pay dividends many times over.

Indecision

Managing requires making decisions, and all decisions involve the use of time and an element of risk taking. Supervisors, like all other leaders, normally do not enjoy or want to make mistakes. Fear of making mistakes—or worse, failing—can and does lead to indecisiveness. Caution or prudence is one thing; indecision is quite another. Sometimes the line between caution and indecision is very thin.

Successful leaders have learned that mistakes will occur in decision making. It is usually better to make a decision and be wrong than not to make a decision at all. The key to avoiding indecisiveness is to gather information quickly, sort and evaluate it quickly, examine the alternatives, weigh the consequences, and then make the decision. Invariably, some decisions will turn out to be wrong. It does not pay to wallow in guilt or self-pity. Use the mistake as a learning experience to guide future decisions.

Procrastination

Most people have a tendency to do a certain amount of procrastinating. There appear to be four major reasons. They are: fear, dislike, boredom, and being overwhelmed. The most significant is fear. Fear can be irrational and it needs to be put in proper perspective. You need to ask yourself: "What is the worst thing that could happen if I did the task improperly? How likely is that to occur?" Quite often we find our fears have been blown out of proportion. People avoid starting tasks or projects either because they do not understand what is required, or the things that need to be done appear confusing. Try breaking the task down into manageable steps or activities that can be readily accomplished.

The unpleasant task is not likely to go away or be carried out on its own accord. If it cannot be delegated or ignored, then it is going to have to be done by *you*. The longer you think about it, the more of a burden it is likely to become. The important thing is to take that first step and begin doing what needs to be done.

It is important to set a deadline. The adage "Work expands to fill the time available" has a lot of truth embodied within it. A sense of urgency causes most people to act. Without a deadline, many important things will not get acted upon. Set a specific, firm deadline. Committing a deadline to others can be especially useful if you are prone to feeling embarrassed when deadlines are not met.

It is also useful to find shortcuts without sacrificing the quality or quantity of results. Shortcuts not only allow us to get more done in less time, they also enable us to get through unpleasant tasks more quickly.

It is important to reward ourselves for progress on unpleasant tasks.

Minibreaks can be useful if we compel ourselves to return to the task at hand. When an unpleasant or undesirable task is completed, it is important to look back and see what was accomplished. It is now time to reward ourselves for successfully completing the task.

Applying the Pareto Principle

The Pareto Principle, named after the Italian economist and sociologist Vilfredo Pareto, has received a lot of attention in recent years with regard to statistical process control and quality assurance. It can also be effectively applied to time management. The Pareto Principle states that the significant items in a given group normally constitute a relatively small portion of the total items in the group. This is commonly referred to as the 80–20 rule. Supervisors may spend 80 percent of their time doing things that generate only 20 percent of the important results, and 20 percent of their time on critical things that generate 80 percent of the important results.

Analyses of how time is being spent and seeing what results were achieved for varying amounts of time used can help you decide if the time was well spent or if changes are in order.

Using Dead Time

So often we find ourselves with dead time on our hands. Dead time is that spent waiting for a call, waiting on someone, being stuck in traffic, standing in line, sitting at an airport, and the like. When we can anticipate dead time will occur, take other work along that does not require intense concentration over an extended period. This is work that can be done quickly, started, stopped, and then picked up again at a later time, or work that is not critical. We often do not know how long the dead time will last, but it can be an excellent chance to catch up on reading for pleasure or business. It can also be a good time to listen to tapes or dictate memos.

Following Your Biorhythm

Each of us has a unique biorhythm. Biorhythm is determined not only by genetic makeup, but also by what we eat and how we live. It is important for us to know something about our biorhythm. Some people do not function well unless they eat a good breakfast—they need their morning coffee or orange juice to get them started. Some people work best under pressure. Some do their best in the early morning hours.

If you are the type of person who cannot function in the morning without first having coffee, then be sure to drink some before working. If you do your best thinking in the evening, stay after regular hours to do serious thinking, get a flexible work schedule, or work at home in the evening. If you think best in the early morning hours, make the most important decisions in the morning.

Managing Details

All jobs require some attention to details. Although higher-level managers often can assign details to others, supervisors usually have to tend to details themselves. The details of any job should be evaluated against objectives, priorities, and job requirements. If you find yourself overburdened with details, present your case to higher management to get clerical, technical, or administrative assistance. Cost-benefit analysis of your time and energy in relation to a nonsupervisory employee's time is necessary to show higher management how time and money can be saved when other employees do some of the detail work.

Delegating to Others

From a time-management perspective, supervisors who delegate work to others increase the results that can be obtained. One person can accomplish only so much; a well-managed group sharing responsibility can accomplish much more. If you delegate to others you also have more time for more important work. Employees who willingly assume responsibility usually gain confidence through achievement and, in effect, become better employees. Better employees cause fewer problems; therefore, supervisors spend less time having to exercise discipline and control.

Understanding Stress

Stress is a fact of modern life. For many reasons, life is more stressful now than in the past. The word *stress* connotes different things to different people. Before any discussion of stress can occur, let's define the word itself: Stress is the nonspecific response of the body or mind to any demand made upon it. From an engineering perspective, loading, which is external, causes stress, which is internal, which leads to strain, which is also internal, which may cause overloading and overstress, which will cause a yielding that can, if not checked, trigger a breakdown or rupture.

People vary widely in their ability to cope with stress. Some have well-developed psychological and physiological mechanisms to deal with a great deal of stress, while others have little capacity to effectively cope with minimal stress.

Stress has been shown to be beneficial. It certainly stimulates the body and mind. It is well accepted that some people work better under stress. It is also well known that, in the absence of stress, some people create stress either on or off the job. Even when job stress is present to a large degree, some people will create more stress. There are two plausible reasons for the phenomena. First, there's a need to negate job-related stress by self-induced stress or risks. People usually have little if any control over dangers in the work place. One way to cope with these is to expose ourselves to dangers over which we have some control. In some way, this may make it easier for a person to cope with job-related dangers. The second reason is a kind of desensitization process. By subjecting ourselves to a lot of stress, it makes stress on the job much easier to handle. In dealing with stress—and for that matter, in successfully living life—the key is to maintain balance. Too much or too little of anything at a specific time can be detrimental and create stress and strain.

First-level management can be a very stressful occupation. The degree of stress and strain varies with the work environment and with each individual's relative ability to cope. Some people need to recognize and accept that they simply do not have the ability to cope with the stress of supervising in certain work situations. Most people can competently handle a high degree of stress for a short duration. Obviously, as the intensity, frequency, and duration increase, people's ability to cope decreases. As stress increases, so does physical and emotional strain. At some point things get out of balance, and signs of stress overload begin to surface. Extroverts show a tendency to release the tension, while introverts bottle it up inside themselves. Sometimes stress builds up in people faster than it can be released. And sometimes it is held inside too long and either takes its toll on the individual's physical health or is released in an extreme manner. It is important for each of us to recognize the signs of stress and strain within ourselves, developing better coping skills and find constructive outlets for high levels of stress.

When people are under considerable stress, they often act in ways far different from their normal patterns of behavior. The normally quiet person either gets extremely quiet and withdrawn, or goes in just the opposite direction. The normally outgoing employee becomes extremely gregarious or does the opposite. Abrupt, dramatic changes in behavior are caused by something; significant changes over time are caused by something. Some changes can be improvements, but when behavior deteriorates, and the deterioration is either prolonged or very bad, a problem exists.

People also need to sense and interpret physiological feedback. Occasional aches and pains are part of everyday living, and often are associated with the aging process. It is when signs are strong or persistent that trouble exists. When our bodies no longer function properly, the problem may be stress related. Clearly, we need to first ask ourselves if our physical problem could be stress related before running to the physician's office. All too often a physician cannot find a physiological cause for real physical problems. When physical cause is absent, look for an emotional cause.

Some physical signs of being under too much stress are:

- Frequent, loose bowel movements
- Chest pains
- Persistent headaches
- Backaches
- Frequent upset stomach or pain in the stomach
- Indigestion and resultant bad breath
- Chronic itching

Any of these signs could be indicative of serious illness, however quite often they are stress related. Reducing the stress often brings the body back to normal.

Some of the emotional signs of being under too much stress are the following:

- You have difficulty remembering things that happened recently; you often forget where you left things; you even forget appointments and meetings.
- You are easily distracted and your attention span has shortened.
- Your mind tends to race off in many directions simultaneously.
- You start seeing things much more negatively than positively.
- You become increasingly rigid and inflexible.
- You show a markedly lower willingness to compromise.
- You start abdicating responsibilities.
- You start to see yourself as a victim; your sense of humor becomes more cynical.
- You become overly demanding.
- You start to fantasize a lot.

Some symptoms of job burnout are the following:

- You start overreacting to things that heretofore didn't bother you.
- You use a lot of energy just to get through the day and leave work feeling totally drained.
- You start asking yourself "Why am I doing this?"
- You start to withdraw from people, including loved ones.
- You have a strong, frequent need to be left alone.
- You feel trapped in your job.

Constructively Managing Stress

Most organizations require that employees take time off from work. It gives people an opportunity to recharge their emotional batteries. Taking a short vacation or a couple of days off away from what is causing stress and strain can be beneficial. It allows a person to stand back, see things clearer, and put them in proper perspective.

It is important to learn how to relax, to disconnect from technology, be it the television, computer, or portable telephone, and not feel guilty about it. Getting out of the house and going for a walk in the woods or somewhere where there are not a lot of people can be healthful and enjoyable. Having sex with someone you love or care deeply about is a well-known beneficial way to reduce stress and strain.

Identify those things in your life over which you have no control and learn to accept them. Too often, people put too much time and energy into trying to change what they really cannot change. Stop worrying over that which you cannot change or control.

Seek occasional solace through prayer and/or meditation. This may be done during the course of the workday, or any other appropriate time. Maintain a healthy outlook on life—life is a precious gift and should be used wisely. Remember, every day above ground is a good day.

Decide what in life is really important to you. Decide what things you have been doing cause stress but provide little meaningful return, and if possible stop doing them.

In our country we continually surround ourselves with things we believe will make us happy. It may be time to ask if these things really do make us happy or if it is all an illusion. It may be time to stop acquiring and start discarding. How many of us buy gadgets, gizmos, and adult toys that are supposed to make our lives easier, but in reality cause more problems than they are worth? How many electronic gadgets are difficult to use, require all kinds of support equipment, are prone to breaking down, are expensive, and sometimes are impossible to repair? Some electronic gadgets are indeed work and time savers; many are not. Decide what will really bring happiness and peace of mind.

It may be time to begin to simplify your life. Get rid of some of your "things" and "stuff" that you needed only because you convinced yourself, or clever marketing convinced you, that you had to possess. It may also be time to reduce your socializing with people whom you do not particularly care for, and to end involvement in activities that you no longer enjoy and no longer truly benefit from.

For some, it may be even time to consider whether the demands of the job are really worth it, relative to the benefits derived. It is better to be in a job that one truly enjoys than to feel trapped in one that pays well but provides little reward beyond the paycheck. Feeling trapped in a job can, and usually is, devastating.

Instead of despairing about too much stress and strain, take a problem-solving approach and plan a course of action. The problem-solving approach is basically the following:

- Analyze the present situation: Where are you now?
- Identify the constraints and givens.
- Establish goals and objectives: Where do you want to end up?
- Consider possible courses of action.
- Decide on a course or courses of action.
- Make and implement the decisions.

When people gain or regain control over their lives and reduce their stress to a manageable level, they achieve these results:

- They learn to accept and better deal with realities.
- They get more enjoyment out of life and relationships with others.
- Their energy level rises.
- Their self-confidence improves.
- They stay healthier longer and live longer.

Index